Eva

Think BIG!

Best.

Philip

AF684952

CHANGE

& How To Survive In THE NEW ECONOMY

All Rights Reserved
© MMVII by LifeSuccess Publishing, LLC

This book may not be reproduced in whole or in part, by any means, without written consent of the publisher.

LIFESUCCESS PUBLISHING, LLC
8900 E Pinnacle Peak Road, Suite D240
Scottsdale, AZ 85255

Telephone: 800.473.7134
Fax: 480.661.1014
E-mail: admin@lifesuccesspublishing.com
ISBN: 978-1-59930-015-3
Cover : LifeSuccess Publishing
Layout: Lloyd Arbour & LifeSuccess Publishing

COMPANIES, ORGANIZATIONS, INSTITUTIONS, AND INDUSTRY PUBLICATIONS: Quantity discounts are available on bulk purchases of this book for reselling, educational purposes, subscription incentives, gifts, sponsorship, or fundraising. Special books or book excerpts can also be created to fit specific needs such as private labeling with your logo on the cover and a message from a VIP printed inside. For more information please contact our Special Sales Department at LifeSuccess Publishing.

CHANGE

& How To Survive In The New Economy

7 Steps to Finding FREEDOM & Escaping the Rat Race

Bob Proctor LIFE SUCCESS PUBLISHING

BARRIE DAY

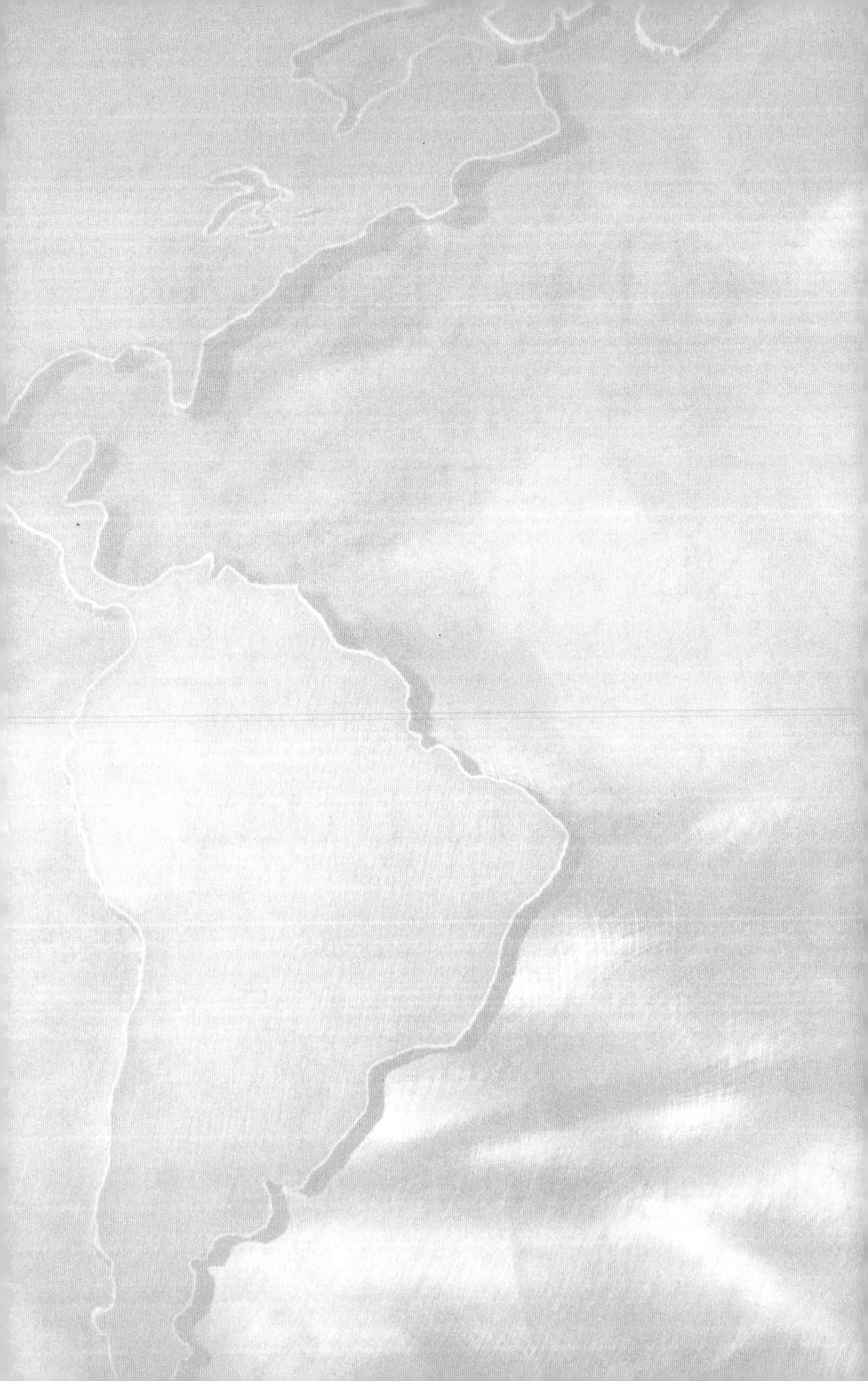

THE SURVIVAL *OF THE FITTEST!*

Are you prepared for the coming economic storm? What does this really mean for the future of America?

Explore the vast conspiracy between government and big business to reduce your income, increase your taxes, and take away your benefits …

… and discover what you can do about it!

If you have been forced out, downsized, outsourced, right-sized, demoted, off-shored, forced to take a pay-cut or even lost your pension, this book is for you!

Find success in the New Economy: create wealth and live the life of your dreams!

– Barrie Day

"Non Sire, c'est une révolution."

Duc de La Rochefoucauld-Liancourt (1747-1827)

"No Sir, it is a revolution."

...in reply to Louis XVI's question, "C'est une revolte?" on hearing of the fall of the Bastille.

This book is for the many faceless citizens whose voices are finally raised in outrage.

CONTENTS

FOREWORD

by Gerry Robert, author of Millionaire Mindset

Writing a book about technology and economics is like writing a book about the Vietnam War. What you write depends a lot on which side you were on, and when. Either way, anything you write will start an argument. The author has written a tough, unbiased view about a number of grave social and economic challenges that the United States faces. These include the economic consequences caused by outsourcing, greedy corporations exploiting the lower-paid workers, and government waste, as well as the cost of the war in the Middle East.

Here, Barrie Day addresses the substantial differences between the rich and the poor of this country and the lack of political backbone to deal with the issues that matter most to people: education, healthcare and employment. He has covered the waterfront and spared no one with the range of issues. Therefore, one would be hard pressed to argue against the facts he presents. This book should prompt a spirited debate at the dinner table and, at the very least, get parents and their children thinking more deeply about the future of the world and what this may mean if they do not act. Some people may become disturbed and even angry over the comments Day makes about this country. I trust they will take the time to understand that this was, in fact, a labor of love by the author for America and Americans. His concerns may mirror the concerns of many of our citizens; however, he has attempted to boldly voice those concerns and, more importantly, he dares to talk about solutions.

ACKNOWLEDGEMENTS

As a long-time resident and business consultant in California's Silicon Valley, I have both observed and have been a party to some huge successes with some of the companies based here. Unfortunately, I have also seen some of the colossal and less-publicized flops that have taken place. This history gives me at least a minimum qualification to comment on some of the issues I see with the birth of the New Economy and also to comment on the stark differences between this economy and previous ones.

As I write about a topic as controversial as this one, I can only hope to avoid intense criticism by saying the selection of the companies listed in the book was based on the criteria that I felt were most representative of the New Economy. I'm sure that by the time this book is published the list will be passé, and even newer and more exciting businesses will be operating.

Therefore, I will take full responsibility for whatever shortcomings this list, though outdated, may entail, and I hope thereby to relieve my publisher of a burden he was less than excited to assume. In the more than two years I spent writing this book, many changes have taken place in the US and globally. Sadly, few of these changes have addressed the most serious issues confronting us. If anything, the challenges have been exacerbated by the political agendas of politicians, the financial interests of big business, and the absence of accurate critical reporting on so many of the events that have taken place. Ben Bradlee, the former editor of *The Washington Post*, once wrote, "The pursuit of truth is a Holy Pursuit, and the business of journalism is to report not what they said happened, not what you think should happen, but what did happen."

As Americans, we cannot escape our responsibility to be well-informed about and involved in our country's actions. While we may live in a dumbed-down culture consisting of celebrity worship, *American Idol* TV shows, and year-round sports, the fact remains that right now a war is being fought by Americans 7,000 miles away, a war that seldom merits more than brief mention in the back sections of our newspapers, usually behind the sports pages and the advertisements. We are in trouble, and the arrogance and ignorance of those in power is frightening to behold.

When writing a book of this scope, there are so many people who have influenced my thinking or contributed in some way that listing all of those who have earned my gratitude becomes an endless litany of names. However, with your patience I would like to thank some of the notables, including James Carville, Lou Dobbs, Paul Krugman, Ron and Anil Hira, Arianna Huffington, Melissa Rossi, Geoffrey Moore, Doug Henwood, and Gerald Swanson. I would be remiss if I did not mention the staff and management of *The Economist* who, with their writings, enabled me to reflect more deeply on the New Economy and its impact on America. I would also like to thank the Harvard Business School and the Paris Summit for some particularly thought -provoking ideas from the participants and faculty, especially *Blue Ocean Strategy* authors W. Chan Kim and Renee Mauborgne.

I am grateful to Kim Medeiros for patient and thoughtful research in spite of storms both literal and metaphorical, as well as Shilpa Verma who, with deep thought and analysis, was able to help shape the intellectual content and any academic merit this book may hold. Also, I should mention Kandi Miller and Gerry Robert, who always provided guidance, kindness, and encouragement in what at times seemed a project without end.

Love and appreciation go to Andrew, Julia, and Stephanie. And I wish to extend a belated acknowledgement to my late father, whose infinite wisdom and deep understanding I sorely miss. I also offer a note of sincere thanks and encouragement to those countless hundreds of thousands of firefighters, nurses, teachers, policemen, waitresses, cooks, ambulance drivers, and the millions of poor everywhere, people of all shapes, sizes and colors who tolerate without complaint, and often operate under, difficult or impossible circumstances created by the inequities discussed in this book. They helped write it; therefore, this book is for them, and now is the time for change!

Finally, no acknowledgement would be complete without my deepest and most sincere thanks to Linda, whose love, encouragement, patience, and timely suggestions helped shape what I trust is a book to help those lost souls find their way in the New Economy.

"There is nothing more difficult to take in hand, more perilous to conduct, or more uncertain in its success, than the introduction of a new order of things."

– Nicolò Machiavelli, *The Prince* (pub. 1515)

Barrie Day
November 2007
Palo Alto, California

INTRODUCTION:

The New Economy…Or How the Rich got Richer!

"So quick bright things come to confusion."

– William Shakespeare,
A Midsummer Night's Dream

This is not a book about politics, although my Republican friends may accuse me of it. Nor is it a book about economics, or big business, or even technology. It is, however, a book about how these four systems are destroying the financial future for many working class Americans and along with it their way of life. This book also discusses some viable solutions to this devastating trend. The question to be answered here is, "How does anyone survive in the New Economy?"

In spite of **extraordinary** corporate profits, broad economic data show that wealth has not been spread evenly throughout our society over the past ten years. There has been an increase in poverty, debt has risen, personal savings rates have fallen, and wages are at a standstill (since 1997 the minimum wage has stayed at $5.15 an hour, although this is at last being discussed in Congress); nevertheless, health care costs are rising, and energy prices and the cost of producing oil have increased along with the cost of housing. Interestingly, in spite of these issues as well as the devastation caused by Hurricane Katrina, in December 2005 members of the US Senate quietly approved a $3,100 a year raise for themselves behind closed doors, boosting their salaries to $165,200 a year. At forty hours a week, that gives Congressmen and women a salary of just under $103 per hour - assuming they work 1600 hours hour per year, which may, in turn, be optimistic!.

America is currently carrying a trillion-dollar deficit which, coupled with all the above, may be the beginning of the biggest financial crisis since 1929. Every hour of every day, the US incurs an additional eighty million dollars of debt; and in three years, this debt will be at eight trillion dollars owed primarily to overseas investors. The Federal Deficit has been the topic of discussion for many years, with many government spokespersons saying there is nothing to worry about. Inflation may not appear to be of concern in the short term, but monetary inflation will be an issue in the long run. Deficits are the fuel for price increases, but this practice of "borrow and spend" is not a sound economic strategy. In 1975 the Gross Federal Debt was $542 billion, today it is $7,900 billion! When countries spend more than they have coming in they have to borrow to cover the difference, just like any typical family. In America today these loans are coming primarily from overseas, primarily from Asia, and specifically from China.

The current low interest rates used to keep the economy going will stimulate the average consumer to spend more. However, these low rates may not be enough to compensate overseas investors for the slide in the value of the dollar. Both the poor economic picture and the hemorrhage of higher-paying jobs have forced banks to provide exotic ways to fuel the economy and provide financing to homeowners as well as to speculators hoping to get some of the returns due to the current housing bubble. As I write this the federal government has just increased interest rates by two points in an effort to attract and maintain foreign investors. However, if the interest rates continue to rise those homeowners who signed up for exotic, interest-only loans, without regard to their income, will be unable to make payments on those loans, which will not only force the price of housing down to more realistic levels but will also bankrupt many current owners. Together with the increase in unemployment, this means there is a real and imminent possibility for one of the largest recessions this country has seen since the 1930's.

Of those who are unemployed, nearly twenty percent have been out of a job for six months or more. More than four million people are working part-time because they can't find full-time work. In spite of record corporate profits, millions of people are getting by on subsistence wages and are seemingly unable to participate in this New Economy. Many people are disillusioned with the government and its failure to prepare for an economy that seems to support wealth over jobs. For the first time these New Economy industries do not require the assistance of clerical, administrative, or support staff in their daily operations. In the future, this trend may also affect engineers as companies consider outsourcing or investing in highly educated, low-wage countries like India and China. That phenomenon appears to be the future for this country. What will our children do for jobs? And what about their children, the ones who will have to service this enormous debt? What does it mean for our educational system? What does it mean for the economic foundation of this country if we are unable to provide stable, long-term, high-paying jobs?

The divisions between the rich and poor have never been wider, thanks to several years of government policies and New Economy business strategies that concentrate wealth at the expense of wages. Also, the rapid evaporation of those aspects we consider essential to a civilized society, such as a high employment rate, health care, Social Security, education, other paid benefits, pollution control, inflation, and programs to eliminate poverty, are now being squeezed between government and business cost-reduction. The result is that our quality of life is in danger of being sharply reduced. There are approximately 6.4 million Americans who rely on both Medicaid and Medicare to pay their medical expenses. Recently, votes were cast in Congress and cuts were announced in health care and college loans in order to give billions in tax breaks to millionaires. The Bible warns in Isaiah 10:2, "Woe to you legislators of infamous laws…who make widows their prey and rob the orphan." Make no mistake. This is both a national crisis and a national shame.

CHAPTER 1

An Economic Revolution: "The times, they are a changing."

"Truth will come to light…in the end truth will out."

– William Shakespeare,
The Merchant of Venice

CHAPTER 1

The year was 1995. William Jefferson Clinton was in the White House. The California, U.S. and world economies were all doing well. It was a time for the lowest unemployment rate in modern times; the lowest inflation in thirty years; the highest home ownership in the country's history; dropping crime rates in many places; and, at last, reduced welfare rolls. It was the first balanced budget in decades; we had even achieved a budget surplus. The times were reminiscent of the Old Economy, with more stable business comprised of large industrial companies typically engaging in mass production and mass marketing. The pace of business was predictable and slow and was often based on a pyramid bureaucratic structure with a large hierarchy. It operated in a traditional, command-and-control type of business model. To a large extent, the economy was based on and fueled by financial capital. The Old Economy companies' business activities were characterized by low volatility (i.e., rate of change) and the payment of dividends, as they had traditionally operated in mature industry sectors.

If we look back at those times not so long ago, the Dow Jones Index was comprised of such companies as Philip Morris, Texaco, Morgan (JP), Chevron, Exxon, DuPont, Minnesota Mining & Manufacturing (3M), International Paper, General Electric, and Eastman Kodak. However, the turbulent change created by technology and innovation was just beginning to impact these giants of industry. In the Dow Jones Index of 1991, Disney replaced US Steel; in 1997 Woolworth was replaced by Wal-Mart; and in 1999 Union Carbide was replaced by SBC Communications, Chevron by Microsoft, and Goodyear by Intel. The shift to a very different economy had begun in earnest among these very different industries.

America has always led the way with new and innovative ways of doing business as far back as the early 20th century. Going even further back in history to the early 1900's, the use of the steam engine, electricity, and open-hearth furnaces allowed business to expand nationwide. Railways also began supplementing the waterways to move goods and people, eventually overtaking them as efficient modes of transportation. By 1910 there was widespread use of the assembly line, and due to staff shortages in the automotive industry, factory wages were doubled and the workday shortened. At the same time, industrial and trade unions doubled membership and were able to increase wages, too. In the 1920's the modern consumer economy was well underway, led by the widespread use of automobiles and new electrical products like the radio and refrigerator. "Talkie" movies made their debut and frozen food became available, further signs that our world had changed forever. It was also a time of strong anti-trust legislation and prosecution.

This was also a time of tax cuts for both corporations and individuals. Union membership would decline sharply at this time, and the minimum wage and maximum working hour standards would be overturned. By the 1930's things had changed dramatically. This was the time of the Great Depression: unemployment averaged twenty-five percent, and union membership began to increase dramatically once again. New technologies such as nylon and fiberglass were developed and made available, and there were major advances in the field of aviation. The next decade brought the onset of World War II and the explosion of military spending. The first computer was built at this time, along with the atomic bomb. With all of these advancements and opportunities, the US inevitably became a global power.

During the 1950's business grew at an amazing rate, possibly due to the huge increase in the population but certainly because of the unleashed demand from the war years. Political concern increased as the Cold War developed, and the focus of military spending shifted to nuclear devices as a form of defense strategy and deterrence. Union membership was at its highest. By the 1960's the economy was booming with color TV's and other consumer electronics, and the Mustang automobile signaled the arrival of the popular, inexpensive, highly-powered "muscle car." Microchips began to appear almost everywhere, along with fast-food chains and the widespread use of antibiotics. It was also a time when factory automation significantly reduced jobs.

The 1970's saw the beginning of the biotech industry and the commercialization of the computer. It was a time of great changes in energy, as OPEC and other oil- producing nations flexed their muscles on pricing even as demand began to skyrocket, which led to an oil embargo and the end of the age of cheap energy. Women were entering the workforce in larger numbers when the start of the service sector of the economy began to eclipse manufacturing as a source of jobs, and the influence of organized labor began to diminish again. The trend away from a jingle large plant towards a multi-location has meant a loss of influence by workers and waving power by the unions.

In the 1980's the decline of labor continued, and the shift to a service economy became even more pronounced. During this time the software and PC industries boomed, and information technology redistributed job functions in the administrative and clerical fields. By the 1990's America's population had reached 280 million, and the economy was again booming. In spite of this boom, the service sector outpaced manufacturing in new job creation; it was a time of record high employment. Despite the modest recession of 2001 and 2002, almost everyone agreed that, based on economic history, technological advances were the main source of economic growth. Some even predicted that these technological advances would *increase* employment and provide better paying jobs for everyone. Interestingly the percentage of women with a child under 6 yrs in the labor force increased from 30% in the seventies to 70% by 2003. The social and cultural consequence of this trend should be of grave concern.

This era introduced new technologies that would have an impact on the country and the world, including the cellular phone, the personal computer, and the Internet. With the advent of these technologies, things were never going to be the same again for the workers of this country. The Old Economy of the past would soon be replaced. It had been comprised of large, well-established, name-brand companies that dominated the economic landscape, usually based in traditional industries such as automotive, manufacturing, and retail. The companies were household names and included Chrysler, General Electric, and Woolworth. They were large, predictable, stable, local and slow. The economic model was based almost exclusively on financial capital and profits. The workforce was characterized by a high proportion of clerical, semi-skilled or unskilled manual workers supervised by better-educated managers, usually holding college degrees. The organizational style was hierarchical, and it emphasized command and control.

In contrast, the New Economy, which was swiftly replacing the Old Economy, involved the heavy use of innovation, technology, the Internet, and knowledge to create fundamentally new business models in areas such as new applications, globalization, communications, new tools, marketplaces, and new technology. The companies in these areas have also become household names; they include such companies as Google, eBay, Cisco and Intel. These New Economy companies are smaller, less predictable, less stable, global and **very** fast, in sharp contrast to their Old Economy predecessors. Their economic model is based on knowledge management, integration, information and communication technology, e-business, computerized design, and interconnected organizational structures that extend to suppliers and customers alike. Likewise, the workforce is characterized by highly technical and advanced science degrees, often in tandem with advanced degrees in business.

The New Economy has created incredible business success stories due to fundamental changes in business operation based on the power of the Internet, new technologies, e-commerce, and global strategies. It has dramatically transformed performance in a wide array of industries. However, it has also changed how Americans live their lives. From 2001 to 2004, the US lost 2.7 million jobs, with 300,000 going overseas and the rest disappearing due to gains in productivity. Every percentage point gain in productivity is a loss of 1.3 million jobs. With productivity growing at an annual rate of more than three percent of all jobs, this means many existing jobs are seriously at risk. At the time this book went to press, Intel had just announced that it would be investing a billion dollars for a Research and Development Center in Bangalore, India, as well as $250 million in local companies. Similarly, Microsoft has made very clear the importance of India to its business plan by announcing a $1.7 billion investment there over the next four years. Furthermore, on a recent visit to Bangalore, Bill Gates, the Chairman of Microsoft, spoke to 5,000 developers and offered an internship with his company for one year to the most promising code developer. In addition public awareness of the costs of the war in Iraq & Afghanastan in both financial and human terms has only just started.

There is a very real risk that America could fall behind in the global brain race. Currently, the USA leads the world in spending on research and development to the tune of approximately $329 billion a year which, although large, represents a flat or declining level of investment in real purchasing power over several years. The level of innovation created by this investment also creates growth in the economy. Since productivity growth determines who the leader is in this global economy, innovation becomes a key aspect of our country's economic strategy.

Engineers, chemists, mathematicians, and physicists are increasingly coming from China and India. Last year China graduated 500,000 engineers, India graduated 200,000 and North America graduated only 70,000. For several years there has been a marked lack of interest in the sciences, which may explain why US high-school seniors recently tested below the international average for twenty-one countries in mathematics and science. Approximately one third of the fourth graders and one fifth of the eighth graders were unable to perform basic mathematical computations. The possibility for future employment may become more and more a matter of advanced degrees and technology, with no alternatives for jobs for our children!

This process has already started. If we look through the classifieds in any provincial newspaper and you'll find job ads for manicurists, hairdressers, and similar low- paying service industry positions only. The consequences of the US-led market-oriented economic policies, which have hurt many Latin America countries with huge debt, hyperinflation, and pervasive unemployment, might be a tell-tale sign of our future. With huge loans from the International Monetary Fund and the US, market-friendly economic policies were implemented overseas, resulting in painful cuts to social programs. Will it happen here?

With 128 million Latin Americans living on less than two dollars a day, inflation hovering at a staggering 2,500% a year, and a shocking twenty-eight percent of Latin Americans being impoverished, it is clear that these economic policies increase the division between rich and poor. These countries were deeply in debt in much the same way that the US is today, with deficits reaching close to six percent of the GDP. The situation becomes even more serious when we realize that the US has the same debt issue to deal with as Latin America along with the impact of the New Economy, too.

In the past, we have blindly accepted that the manufacturing industries of this country and the blue-collar jobs that accompany them would migrate to countries with less expensive labor, however, currently, there are major layoffs also in the administrative and clerical areas in functions such as technical support and call centers, among others. If the research and development jobs are also going abroad, what is left for Americans to do? What does it mean for families ill-equipped for these changes? The government has been a supporter of this tragic strategy, due mainly to heavy industrial lobbying, and may still not have grasped the implications of its actions.

When ones examines the concept of a redistribution of wealth in areas such as our healthcare system. The most profound changes in the world economy have taken place over the past 20 years. There has been a dramatic reduction in the growth of income per person in the low and middle-income group.

At a country level world income distribution 30 years ago could expect income per person to increase by 67% in 20 years. In 1980 the figure was only 22%.

In a country as the U.S. the case could be made that we could reduce poverty and unemployment and improve the quality of life through redistribution of wealth.

Given the current state of our healthcare system is largely in private hands, one wonders whether powerful lobbyists were able to obtain the vote in their favor to change the system. Back in 1989 a similar situation developed when a savings and loan executive was able to influence US senators to intervene on his behalf with federal regulators after donating $1.3 million to their political war chests. The subsequent collapse of this savings and loan company cost taxpayers over $2.6 billion. Again recently we have seen members of Congress attempting to influence Interior Secretary Gale Norton regarding Indian casinos while in return receiving $830,000 for their political war chests. It seems that members of Congress are too cozy with various special interest groups at the expense of their constituents. This has become a multibillion-dollar influence-peddling industry that is far too loosely tracked and regulated.

In the above example of healthcare lobbying, it is expected that these lobbying expenses will reach $325 million for the various health care providers, insurers, drug makers, and pharmaceutical companies who depend on favorable legislation to maintain their current profit levels. Interestingly, many of these same lobbyists were instrumental in writing and selling the laws ultimately passed by those who received these funds. To quote Melanie Sloan, who now runs Citizens for Responsibility & Ethics in Washington, D.C., a group that monitors public officials' conduct, "Special interests do get more, and they do get what they pay for despite the constant denial that lawmakers can't be bought." Otherwise, why would they continue to lobby? The revolution in corporate behavior arguably began with the Republican takeover of Congress in 1994, when several outspoken GOP leaders demanded that business groups support the party not only by contributing to campaigns but also by selecting party faithful to run trade associations. The accounting profession gave more than half of its campaign donations to Democrats in 1994. However, by the middle of 2005 they had given seventy-one percent to Republicans. Similarly, the insurance industry increased its donations to Republicans to sixty-eight percent in the same decade. Energy interests increased the share going to Republicans from sixty-four to seventy-five percent a decade later. With the help of Trent Lott of Mississippi, the Senate Majority Leader at the time, even the scrap metal dealers were able to get off the hook for millions of dollars in potential liabilities at toxic waste sites by donating $300,000 to political candidates.

When the Democrats were in power they played the same game. For example, when President Clinton signed into law "the most significant advancement for people with disabilities," he also enacted, as part of the same bill, a lucrative tax break for banks, insurers, and financial services companies. This tax break would cost the US treasury $1.5 billion over a two year period. Savings and loans, major pharmaceutical companies, automotive companies, energy interests, and healthcare are all aggressively taking care of business - *their* business rather than yours!

In this New Economy without jobs or a realistic income, people are unable to buy the things that have most recently kept the economy afloat during the past recession. With the country's debt burden of eight trillion dollars, the government has to find money to pay its creditors overseas. However, if there are fewer jobs then income taxes are significantly reduced, and the only way forward is to print more money. This will, in turn, lead to hyperinflation without major policy changes and controls in the overall economic policy of this country. The government's recent action of giving people tax breaks was not really giving anyone more money. The government has no money other than what is collected in tax revenues – unless it prints it. More money chasing a fixed level of goods and services is the classic economic definition of inflation.

So, what happened? Back in the early 1990's the stock market was going up, businesses were profitable and growing, and people had decent, well-paying jobs.

However, take a look at the following trends:

- Today the government is running record twin budget deficits
- We engage in a costly war in Iraq and Afghanistan with no end in sight
- Oil has doubled in price
- The U.S. stock market appears to be over-valued.
- Health and retirement benefits are being cut
- Medicare and Medicaid costs are increasing
- Layoffs are continuing to occur
- The dollar continues to slide against most major currencies
- The U.S. houseing market is in a state of collapse
- Several major banks have announced significant losses due to write-downs of leveraged loans.

If we follow these events over time it is clear that there is an economic cycle in place, and this current economic cycle favors investment capital over employees. However, if we examine the trend from as far back as the Agricultural Age through to the Industrial Age and then to the Old Economy, which was predominantly driven by the service industry, there has ***never been a significant reduction in the need for employees,*** whether it be in the administrative, manufacturing, management, or research and development fields. Until now.

In fact, if this trend continues a dramatic change in the overall demographics of the US economy will take place, with a significant number of people being unemployed during their entire lifetimes. Or, this could mean that our children will be employed in menial jobs at minimum wage unless there are major changes in business strategy and government policies in education and taxes. How many nail salons and fast food establishments can the nation afford? Our future depends on refocusing and understanding the broader impacts of our concepts of economic growth.

The USA has typically spent more than it earned, invested more than it saved, and borrowed continuously from overseas investors to make up the difference. As part of this process the USA has repeatedly created new innovative forms of credit with the help of financial institutions, who have been only too happy to loan money to the growing markets of consumers who had the money to spend on goods and services at high interest rates to fuel the economy. Until today this has been the economic policy of this country. However, this economic strategy cannot continue indefinitely. Somehow there must be the necessary changes in our educational systems and our fiscal policies to protect current employees and their jobs over the short-term benefit of corporate profits through the usual tools of layoffs, cutting benefits, and outsourcing offshore.

As an example, our company recently completed some technology consulting and change management work with a major Fortune 500 corporation on the east coast implementing a new Global Information System. As part of that effort we were requested to also implement a Help Desk to support the entire organization. The requisite candidates were found and trained over a two-week period. The candidates were single mothers, the unemployed, some students, and others of like situation. It should be noted that no one had prior experience or a background in high technology. The reference material developed to assist these new employees in this new approach was intentionally written to be easy to learn and digest. The experiment was a marked success. However, the client continued with its outsourcing plans to India because this was "the company policy." If we consider for one moment the consequences of this policy then how can this policy truly make a better or stronger America, with US citizens losing their jobs to less expensive countries?

Based on our success with this small but important effort in sourcing domestically, one wonders if it would be possible to bring back work outsourced to India and at the same time improve ***this*** country's economy and individual wealth. We believe that sometimes the government must also take action to protect its citizens and the country from global corporations interested only in short term profits. In Europe there has been an effort to involve the workers, management, and local government in major strategies and policies in an effort to ensure balance between growth and the quality of life. Where there was a need to reduce costs and possibly lay off workers, this was a joint decision that considered the overall impact on the local economy as well as the corporation. In too many cases US corporations are simply eliminating jobs, along with benefits and pensions, for short-term profit. As has been shown, it ***is*** possible to educate and employ local people, even for these New Economy-type positions.

CHAPTER 2

The New Economy ... And Darwin's Theory in Action

"There is strange toward.... Pray you be careful."

– William Shakespeare,
King Lear

CHAPTER 2

If you are like most Americans, the far reaching changes described here may not have been that apparent. The largest five businesses in the world, according to *The Economist*, are actually still American; they are GM, Wal-Mart, Exxon Mobil, Ford Motor Company, and Daimler Chrysler. You may have noticed that three of the five are in the automotive sector. Yet we see that these companies are, in fact, laying off employees. Interestingly enough, both Toyota and Honda are expanding and building new factories in this country. Maybe the answer for the future lies in the level of innovation. The total expenditure on research and development as a fraction of GDP for the United States is 2.6%, which sounds healthy enough; however, when we also see that Sweden, Finland, Japan, and even Israel spend an even larger fraction of their GDP's on research and development it raises questions regarding our future in this New Economy.

If we examine another aspect of innovation, namely the number of patents granted each year, we find that Japan has literally doubled the number of US patents! The one area in which the US is leading the world is crime and punishment. The rate of incarceration in the US is the highest in the world at 702 per 100,000 people! One wonders why we excel in this category and not in other, nobler causes. However, we are not beating the world in education, healthcare, benefits, homelessness, poverty, pollution, or even longevity. A recent study showed that a Japanese woman born in 1947 could expect to live only fifty-four years while American women at that time had a life expectancy of 68.4 years. By 2001, Japanese women had added an impressive increase of thirty years and can now expect to live to eighty five. The Japanese have kept the record, and interestingly enough the US is not even in the top ten today. We are currently ranked twenty-fifth in longevity, beaten by Japan, Iceland, Canada, France, and Hong Kong. Even Cuba and Barbados were able to make a better show of performance than we were.

The changes above have been very gradual. They have been so gradual you may not have even noticed them. You had a job, sometimes with benefits or even possibly a pension. Sure, you paid taxes, but that was only to be expected. Maybe your partner also worked, which enabled you and the family to take those much needed vacations. But somehow the money does not go as far as it used to.

Yet there were and are plenty of new companies. In the case of Google, which was founded just seven years ago, the company has fundamentally changed the way that people live and work. The company has experienced incredible growth, and the stock traded at almost $509 per share in November 2006. However, the jobs Google has added are highly specialized and technical and require very specific education and training.

The forces driving this New Economy are:

- Knowledge - intellectual capital is a strategic factor;
- Change - which is continuous, rapid and complex;

- Globalization - in every facet of a business, resulting in new economies, such as in India and China, global hyper-competition, and the interdependency of business.

- Technology – convergence and new applications

This volatility in the economy has placed huge demands on individual companies to radically change their ways of doing business. The lifecycles of products are reduced dramatically. (Consider the I-pod). The products themselves are much more customer- driven, and as these products become more of a commodity the need for differentiation becomes essential.

This, in turn, means that the companies operating in the space of the New Economy are much more opportunity-driven and are based on flexibility, technology, and new business models on an almost continuously changing basis. Equally, the work force, such as it is and will continue to be, is multi- skilled, flexible, and based on cooperation and teamwork. With technological breakthroughs, economic growth overseas, market evolution, shifts in customer tastes, and social and political changes, this is the huge potential represented by the New Economy and the strategic and technology innovators in the future. Therefore, it is our contention that the future will belong to those most able to be independent and adapt.

"It's not the strongest nor the most intelligent of the species that survive; It is the one most adaptable to change."

– Charles Darwin

The growth we referred to earlier is chaotic and seemingly random at times; however, it is precisely because of this type of discontinuous change that these new industries could be created, and because of their creation they have helped to accelerate global economic growth that further accelerates the rate of chaotic change.

In this process, older, less adaptive companies have fallen by the wayside. The successful companies in the New Economy have understood that along with a customer-driven economy, knowledge is a major source of value. Globalization led the way to reducing the costs of products; however, information technology enabled them to find and analyze competing products and to make intelligent choices. Therefore, those who understood these factors and who were able to create, find, and combine knowledge into new products and services faster than their competition became the winners. The simultaneous evolution of the Internet provided new ways of building and delivering products and services online. The ability to access vast amounts of information instantly and to communicate globally over huge distances at incredibly low cost is transforming the way people think and work.

In this New Economy we see a vastly different world in which technology, speed, intangibles, and connectivity dominate. However, it is less a place of employment than an incubator of ideas. The constituents will be mostly technologists and marketers, with the other functions increasingly performed overseas as part of this global economy. In this world of boundless information and seamless electronic commerce in the US, people in 2003 responded to these changes with sixty-one percent of listed companies being started at home, with sixteen percent initially capitalized with less than $1,000.

In 2003 entrepreneurs started 572,900 businesses nationwide, although 554,800 firms also closed that year and 35,037 went bankrupt. However, it can also be seen that while this demonstrates the innovation and entrepreneurship of the American people, the same job opportunities and benefits are not available to replace those laid off by GM, Ford, Merck, Hewlett Packard, United Airlines, and other large global corporations.

In November of 2005 GM announced the layoff of 30,000 workers and the closing of twelve plants over the next three years. Ford Motor Company announced that it, too, would be making cutbacks in jobs as part of a restructuring. Delphi Corporation, the largest American automotive parts maker, has outlined a series of changes for their rank-and-file workers, including a sixty-five percent wage cut, an end to overtime pay, a tenfold increase in out of pocket expenses for health care, and the freezing of pension benefits.

The US automobile companies responded slowly to the initial Japanese challenge in the 1980's and became dependent on the high profits generated from the sale of large SUV's and trucks. However, in their focus on the short term they completely failed to anticipate both the tastes of the consumer for superior European and Japanese imports and the current high price of gasoline. More recently Toyota and Honda were the first to market gas-electric hybrids, even though Washington lavished generous subsidies on Detroit in the 1990's to develop these cars. All this and there still has been no real success, or even significant attempt, by American auto manufacturers to produce more fuel-efficient vehicles! Is it any wonder that the US automotive industry is in turmoil?

Of even greater interest is the fact that Toyota is building two more plants in the United States and Canada. One wonders if there is a future for this basic U.S. industry on which so many communities depend for their livelihood and economic well-being.

Questions are rightly being asked of the oil companies whose profits have been excessive and estimated at over $10 million due to

2005's Hurricane Katrina, alone. It has now become clear that the CEO's of these oil companies are also the ones who met secretly with Vice President Dick Cheney to develop an energy policy for this country. One wonders if they recommended an alternative approach, a different strategy, and a creative plan for the use of alternative energy forms such as ethanol, methane, or hydrogen. Did they even discuss a return to enforcing a reduced speed limit on highways in an effort to curb demand, given that the world's leading consumer is the United States with a demand of over 20.5 million barrels per day, of which 8.5 million is for the automobile industry? Additionally, the number of SUV's and Hummers with their low fuel efficiency needlessly stretches this demand even further.

Equally, US Airways (the nation's seventh largest airline, which filed for bankruptcy in August 2005 after losing $2.1 billion in 2001) initiated layoffs, reductions in benefits, pay cuts of thirteen percent, and changes to work rules that will save the airline more than $1.2 billion a year as part of a negotiated settlement. The airline planned to lay off another 2,700 workers in April 2003. From 2003 to 2005 the airline cut 14,000 jobs. In addition to the direct cuts, workers and retirees lost thousands of dollars each from their 401(k) retirement plans that were invested in company stock, since the reorganization plan from the company makes no provision for $3.1 billion in payments owed to the company's pension plan over the next seven years. Yet the top executives were given $6M after bankruptcy as a retention bonus! As a comparison, a flight attendant with twenty-seven years of service makes $9.40 an hour. Starting pay is $6.40 an hour! A similar picture is emerging at United Airlines and American Airlines, who both indicated their intentions in the future to reduce benefits, cut pay, and enact significant layoffs.

In fact, in a devastating blow to 122,000 workers and retirees of United Airlines a federal bankruptcy judge recently ruled that United Airlines might default on its pension obligations of $9.8

billion, the largest default in US history. It represents a staggering $267,000 for every pilot, flight attendant, and mechanic. This event may not be confined to United Airlines and may also include Delta, Northwest, American, and Continental. Of the 30,000 employer plans insured by the federal Pension Benefit Guaranty Corporation, almost sixty percent are underfunded. Again, we can see that often the Old Economy companies fail to respond to the changing times other than to reduce their operating costs. New airlines such as Virgin, Jet Blue, and Southwest are somehow able to take care of their employees as well as remain profitable for their shareholders. Is it because these new companies are using new innovative business models, or maybe just because they value their customers? Perhaps their CEOs are less greedy?

Despite economic growth of 3.8% in 2004, the median household income and wages fell, the number of Americans living below the poverty line (37 million) rose by 1 million, and more Americans went without health insurance (15.7%). The number lacking insurance increased by 800,000 to 45.8 million people. Slowly, globalization is taking a toll throughout the American middle and working classes, shutting down factories and reducing income and benefits.

The government, in response, has passed a bill cutting $50 billion in aid from Medicaid, food stamps, and student loan programs, and it has also resisted an increase in the minimum wage, passed significant tax cuts for the richest one- percent of Americans, and now plans to reduce Social Security payouts. Maybe we can learn something from the Europeans. They retire five years earlier than in the US and have twenty-six days of fully paid vacation a year, compared with the US norm of sixteen days paid vacation.

Clearly Congress, with its comfortable salaries, generous health insurance plans, and secure pensions, is out of touch with the issues affecting America. So where is the economic growth if it isn't showing up in wages? It's going to **huge** corporate profits (largely untaxed), to rising health care costs, and to a surge in the salaries and other compensation of executives. (*Forbes* reports that the combined compensation of the chief executives of America's largest companies rose fifty-four percent in 2005.)

A similar story appears in the financial world. On Wall Street, bonuses were "expected to soar in 2006," with an average pay packet of $2.2 million to $3.3 million for an investment banker and with a global head of investment banking earning anywhere between $7 million and $10 million a *year*, an amount which represents an increase of twenty to twenty-five percent over the year before.

In the following chapters we will examine these New Economy companies to better understand the paradigm changes that have enabled them to be so successful. Equally important, we will highlight the consequences for workers in the future if they wish to survive in a jobless economy or one where income is significantly reduced.

CHAPTER 3

Economic Growth: A Taxing Question for Some

"O foolish youth! Thou seek'st the greatness that will overwhelm thee."

– William Shakespeare,
Henry IV

CHAPTER 3

No one questions the wisdom of growth anymore. The growth experienced by the US in the past enabled it both to help and to influence many other countries, as well as to provide a stable base for its own citizens with gainful employment and a living wage.

Economics is defined as the study, description, and analysis of the ways in which societies produce and distribute goods and services. Adam Smith is considered the founder of modern economics with his theory of the market first published in 1776 in *Wealth of Nations*, a theory based on reduced government interference in the workings of the economy as the key doctrine. However, John Maynard Keynes, another more contemporary economist, examined capitalism and came up with quite different answers, namely that the government needed to spend to stimulate the economy.

For growth to take place, there are a number of conditions that must be met:

- Large and expanding markets
- Technological advances
- The availability of financial capital as investment

- Supply Chain Management to enable fast and cost effective delivery of products and services, and

- "Technology-experienced" resources and consumers

Recent growth has changed the US economy dramatically. Now the richest five percent of the US population owns almost eighty-two percent of corporate stock and controls fifty-seven percent of the net worth of ALL the people in the United States! As *The Economist* magazine reported in a 1999 issue, "Whereas the average earnings of the top fifth of US male earners rose by four percent between 1979 and 1996, those of the bottom fifth fell by forty-four percent." Back in 1980, the average CEO of a large US corporation earned forty-two times that of the average US worker. However, by 1999 market growth had increased that inequality to a point where the average CEO was making *475 times* what the average worker earned. This raises the following question: Has the economic strategy used by recent governments had the trickle down effect envisaged? Providing additional tax breaks to the wealthiest individuals has allowed further distortion to the inequality between rich and poor.

Does this matter? The wealthy argue that they provide the capital and are therefore entitled to the rewards. Is this true? Most people are aware that individual consumers spending their money, not wealthy business owners, made the last recession less painful. If we look at a period of rapid global economic growth from 1960 to the present we see that salary inequality grew, and we also see that the rate of environmental destruction increased; therefore, most thinking people would say our quality of life has diminished.

After the end of World War II the US was one of the most powerful countries on the planet, and it paved the way for US corporations to move their production facilities, materials sourcing, and labor to lower wage areas of the world. This free market approach by the major corporations that was aided and abetted by our own government reduced democratic control over capital. This translates into shifting the tax burden from the large corporations to workers and the small business sector. Since the US started opening its markets in the form of various trade pacts, we have seen the rapid decline of our manufacturing industry, the reduction of average wages, growing income inequality, an increase in the average work week, a significantly increased deficit in the US balance of trade, and a growing mountain of debt (government, consumer, and corporate) that has artificially pumped up the US economy. With so much work being done offshore, this has also improved the overall profitability of corporations; however, this has typically not led to an increase in tax revenues. Reality is quite the contrary. In the 1950's, for every dollar paid in federal, state and local taxes by families, corporations paid eighty cents; but by the 1990's that rate had dropped to twenty-one cents. If one looks at individual taxes contrasted with corporate taxes he sees that while corporate taxes have increased only slightly, individual taxes have gone through the roof! In fact, during the two Reagan administrations the Federal Government accumulated more debt *than during all previous administrations combined.* The interest alone on this debt is $400 billion per year, and because so much of our debt is now held by foreign governments, these interest payments represent capital flight.

During the first three years of President George W. Bush's administration, non-defense discretionary spending of the federal government rose twenty percent. This figure far exceeded the first three years of the previous six administrations. Thanks to the massive tax cuts for the wealthy, federal tax revenues as a percentage of the US economy fell to their lowest level since 1959. For the future, unless social programs are severely cut back there appears to be no alternative to increased taxes on individuals.

This also raises legitimate questions about other quality of life conditions for America. Scholars have written about the limits to growth. However, so far no one has written about the costs of not defining an economic model that is based on wealth and employment with a supporting infrastructure of education and healthcare benefits. Far too many people are homeless, live close to toxic waste sites, are unemployed, or are in need of healthcare. Their future and their children's futures must be weighed in the economic equation of what America will stand for as a nation.

CHAPTER 4

Technology and Rapid Change: Strap Yourself In!

"O the difference of man and man."

– William Shakespeare,
King Lear

CHAPTER 4

In 1990 the first Internet browser was introduced, and by 1994 a company called Netscape was formed because of the belief that there would soon be an explosion in demand for Internet access. This was not to be at this time. In fact, there was a general meltdown of many of these companies in the year 2000, and many companies went bankrupt. However, as is often the case, this bubble was followed by a period of growth. Within three years, 580 million people, thirty percent of them in the US and another sixty percent in Europe and Asia, had access to the Internet. The worldwide Internet population in 2004 was 934 million, with a projection that this will have increased to 1.21 billion by 2006 with 139 million of them (or almost fifty percent of the population) in the US. Internet penetration in the US has reached nearly seventy-five percent of households, rising nine points in one year. Of this number, 44 million are over fifty-five years of age.

This explosion of technology and capability has led to a revolution in many different areas of our lives with mechanization of processes, web logs (known colloquially as "blogs"), discussion boards, e-mail, voicemail, videoconferencing, cell phones, online banking, and other new services added daily. This relatively low-cost, high-speed, global reach Internet operating 24/7 is a major reason the New Economy has become so successful. Most people have an e-mail account these days. Most commercial enterprises have their own web sites, but now even families and individuals have web logs which provide a new way of communicating efficiently with friends and colleagues near and far. This new technology also brought with it some major issues, such as viruses, hackers, spam, and a confusing lack of standards. The gift of technology has provided us with new and different ways of working and thinking and also with new ways of feeling frustrated.

When we are about to make a major purchase, we now tend to do some basic research using tools such as Google, or we might join chat rooms to learn of others' experiences with the product or service we are considering. We are provided with a powerful means of choice and evaluation. Other companies, such as Amazon, are even able to store our preferences and use complex algebraic equations to help us select similar books or music according to our tastes. Many of these paradigm changes are socially beneficial. However, these technological innovations do not seem to provide one of the most basic needs of Americans: jobs.

As we have seen throughout history, there has been this continuous drive for improvement; therefore, change is part of our heritage. The question here is whether the complete system is in synchronization. If there are fewer jobs available in the future and those jobs are significantly different from the existing population's skill sets and education, how are we to progress as a nation? Without the government providing incentives or tax cuts, it is unlikely that big business will discontinue the strategy of exporting jobs overseas.

This in turn forces another question: what should our schools be doing to educate our children for the opportunities of the future? Clearly, the traditional jobs as we know them will not be around. Will high school courses in innovation, technology, Far Eastern languages, and intellectual flexibility replace conventional English, history, and gym?

Maria Klawe, a former dean at Princeton University, wrote this of her concern:

> *"The future of the US information technology industry, and thus the competitiveness of the nation, are caught in a trap of misperception. Since the burst of the dotcom bubble in 2000, young people have avoided careers in information technology. The number of computer science majors at US universities has plummeted. Yet the demand for people with computer science skills is at an all-time high. What is more, computing-related jobs are no longer an isolated component of American industries; IT underpins every function of the business community - market research, product design, finance, strategic planning, environmental issues - every aspect of doing and leading."*

In spite of this demand, US public corporations are increasingly turning to low-cost countries such as India for their resources. In part, this is our own fault. During the 1950's more graduates were awarded Master's Degrees in engineering than in business management. However, by the 1980's MBA's outnumbered engineers by more than three to one. This translated into roughly 64,200 degrees being awarded. Other countries such as Japan were not so quick to copy this trend and continued to emphasize the importance of engineering and computer science to their country's fundamental growth. Clearly, the changes described here are nothing short of revolutionary for the individuals living in this country.

The speed with which these changes are taking place is crippling for the elderly and the less educated. It also leaves the poor and unemployed with fewer opportunities than ever before and qualifies them for little other than menial, low-paying jobs. Is this the country our forefathers intended for us to inherit? If technology is the engine of growth, how can it be used intelligently and as a part of a broad economic program which benefits not only large corporations but also the average citizen? Our goal should be to build a country of opportunity and promise with decent and affordable healthcare, a working school system, and full employment in this New Economy. In the early 1960's when John Kennedy stated his vision of being the first country to put a man on the moon, the innovation and energy of the country were used for the accomplishment of this seemingly impossible task. Can this same energy be created in these difficult economic times to achieve a similar mission?

CHAPTER 5

Paradigm Shift – Toward the New Economy

"We are such stuff as dreams are made of . . ."

– William Shakespeare,
The Tempest

CHAPTER 5

"Our success lies in the secret of our unique business model" was a phrase heard one too many times during the 1990's. And this is rightfully so. From Webvan to Yahoo to Dell, the last phase of the 20th century was an era for entrepreneurs. With the US economy emerging from a partial recession and the popularity of the Internet increasing, everyone with an idea wanted to explore and exploit the new emerging economy.

In the coming years, students of business will ask how an industry icon such as General Motors could slide so quickly from being one of the pillars of American industry into a position of near-bankruptcy. They might wonder: What was this emerging economy? Were the business models really that different from their traditional counterparts? And, more importantly, from the myriad new startups why did only a few succeed? Is the secret answer really the unique business model?

This chapter attempts to explain the distinctive challenges posed and opportunities created by the New Economy.

SUCCESS IN THE PAST	SUCCESS IN THE NEW ECONOMY
Consistenc	Flexibility
Routine	Innovation
Size	Lean
Hierarchical Control	Open
Rational Logic	Tolerance for Ambiguity
Tried & True Approach	New Idea
Cultural Conformity	Cultural Diversity

Courtesy "Finding Your Own North Star" by Martha Beach

For clarity this chapter is divided into two broad sections. We will begin the discussion with a brief look at the evolution of the Internet and how the era demanded change. The second phase of the discussion attempts to understand the evolution of the Old Economy to the New Economy in relation to their business rules.

PART ONE. THE EVOLUTION OF THE TECHNOLOGY CONTINUUM AND CHANGE

The evolution of technology includes both the development of the science defined by the term as well as the meaning of the term itself. Assuredly, this previous sentence does not make much sense by itself. But consider it in this context: What would the word technology mean to a thirty-year-old person working during the industrial revolution? His answer, in all likelihood, would be, "The steam engine."

Now fast forward to the 21st century and ask the same question to a thirty-year old and he would know that technology at its best can be seen in products such as Blackberry, the iPod, Tablet PCs, or in services such as VOIP. The response varies because the word technology, in very simple terms, means "applying the theoretical knowledge base to create a product that decreases manual labor required to perform a task, consequently increasing productivity and efficiency," and with every passing time frame the word "technology" has had a different meaning.

The Internet's influence on the modern world has been what the steam engine was for the Industrial Revolution. The steam engine took us from manual labor to mechanical systems that do the work for us. The invention of the computer chip took us from mechanical to electronic business, and the evolution of the Internet takes us to the next level in the continuum: E-Business. Not only has it changed the way we communicate, but its presence has also redefined businesses. Visionaries who could look beyond the horizon have created companies, the success stories of which will be remembered and studied in times to come.

Behind every company there is a story, a story of how the company changed the business within the industry or the story of how the company drove itself into bankruptcy. The one common factor intertwined in every story of the mature 20th century and the juvenile 21st century is change. Change has been the New Economy's only constant.

Before we look at stories that define the New Economy and how they redefined business, let's take a quick look at how this whole idea of change, or rather paradigm shift, started. The evolution has been very gradual, in fact, spanning three decades. Many attribute this to the invention of the microchip; while this is technically true, we attribute this to the invention of the ARPANET in 1969.

Certainly the microchip allowed for faster computations and better computers, but had it not been for the invention of the ARPANET the Internet either would not have emerged or it would have emerged years later.

ARPANET had been designed for the military to enable scientists to share information. When first introduced, the traffic on the system was very light, and many users thought it was too complex to have any future. It was not until 1983 when ARPANET, and all networks attached to it, adopted the TCP/IP protocol that the Internet as we know it today was born. Of course, after this time the growth of the Internet was exponential, and the system that was once designed to share information among a select few is now moving towards changing how the world communicates and does business everywhere.

The commercialization of the Internet could not have come at a better time. The Internet was introduced to the masses when the world was emerging from a global recession, and everyone from every walk of life was looking for that silver lining in the recessionary clouds. And sure enough, the silver lining emerged in the form of the Internet.

The Internet not only showed us new ways to communicate and gather knowledge, but more importantly, its very presence has actually made our world quite small. Globalization is often thought of as a phenomenon that has mandated companies to change their business models. We like to think of globalization as a phenomenon that was a consequence of the Internet Era.

The Internet Era allowed companies to access consumers across national borders. As proven by the success stories of companies like Amazon.com and eBay, one of their biggest strengths was their capability to meet consumer demands in countries a world away from the United States of America. With international trade flourishing on the Internet, respective governments had to take notice of it and re-write related laws. In addition to accessing customers, the Internet also allowed businesses to search for service providers beyond their regional base. This further increased trade and transparency, once again mandating globalization.

Off-shoring, a subject that continues to be stimulate debate, is a natural consequence of the Internet. While the Internet grew by leaps and bounds, government and businesses were able to take advantage of this development to stimulate trade across national borders without regard to local employment conditions. In addition to crossing national borders, the technological developments of the 1990's challenged the ground rules of traditional business practices and economics. Though often considered synonymous with each other, change and paradigm shift are distinctly different. A paradigm shift refers to a fundamental modification of the thought process, whereas change is a generic term applicable to any deviation from a known form. For example, switching from "LIFO" to "FIFO" for inventory valuation is a change in the method of inventory valuation. However, the understanding that "until it's sold inventory is actually a liability and not an asset" (a pattern of thinking that is exactly the opposite of what was once believed) represents a paradigm shift within the fundamentals of accounting and business practice. This is what the technology period did to our world. Technology did not just change our world, it fundamentally altered how we live and think.

Technological advances demanded change from those who wanted to succeed in this changing economy. So great were the expectations from the technology (Internet) era that companies with negative cash flow had higher market capitalization than the giants of yesterday. For example, Yahoo Inc. was trading at approximately $120 per share compared to the $40-$50 range for General Motors. Although these two companies belong in different types of industries, the promise of technology had even the most savvy business minds in awe. As a result, stock markets soared with the Dow Jones touching the 10,000 mark, and NASDAQ [1] reaching the magical 5000 mark, based solely on future expectations of the emerging technologies. Besides business, the new era had baffled the economists of the country, as well. From simple concepts of the inverted yield curve and low inflation to complex fundamentals of the law of diminishing returns evolving into the law of increasing returns, the new era's business model was perplexing.

While the companies were enjoying glory days and economists were busy trying to understand why the traditional rules were being challenged, something happened. The Internet bubble crashed. After the sudden crash, what resurfaced was the conventional objective for all businesses: profitability. Common sense tells us that the very act of doing business and achieving profitability go hand-in-hand.

The sudden fall in the world financial markets allowed the opponents of the Internet Era to have the last laugh. Instead of the high notes of optimism, there was now talk about bankruptcies and closures. Anything that represented the New Economy was rejected, and once again the cautious approach to investing took focus. It reconfirmed that investors are willing to bet on technology only for so long. Even a company such as Amazon.com, which continued to show increased revenue but NOT profit, could not hold the interest of Lehman Brothers analyst Holly Becker, who changed the recommendation on the stock from a buy to neutral in a report titled "Throwing in the Towel on Amazon." [2] These are very strong words, clearly suggesting that the investing community was losing patience. Amazon.com chief Jeff Bezos was confident that his business model would show profitability soon, but it was not soon enough. This report actually forced Amazon.com to look at the business side and meet the market's profit expectations.

Darwinian logic says nature always evolves. Expanding this, if the New Economy was an evolution of the Old Economy then why was it considered so different? Was it really different, or was there a missing link to the puzzle that everyone overlooked? Technologies which had only recently been highly ranked were being written off instead. Why? Could it be that the missing link would be found in the time-tested principles of the old economy?

PART TWO. OLD ECONOMY TO NEW ECONOMY: BUSINESS RULES REDEFINED

The Old Economy, as we all know, was centered on making profits and meeting stock market expectations. Is it any different today? Not really. The recent trend of dividend buybacks and stock repurchases to meet equity market expectations is a current example of things not being any different today. What *has* changed, though, is the concept of the word "value." Though still competitive, businesses today are trying to adopt cooperative competition as their strategy rather than the gas station price war strategy. For the average consumer this means more value per dollar spent. That which constitutes additional value varies from industry to industry. For the automotive industry this means better warranties, whereas in electronics this means longer lasting batteries. And for the consumer items it could mean something as simple as the bundling of two products at a competitive price.

Another prevalent trend of the 90's era was mergers and acquisitions, or M&A. While some mergers proved successful, some are still trying to succeed to date. Daimler-Chrysler was a merger that created waves across the industry. There was talk of synergies and value addition at the customer level, but as we all know, the promised synergies have culminated in recent announcements of layoffs by the company. With many other similar examples and the rise of interest rates, investment advisors and businesses alike came to realize that mergers on paper don't necessarily translate to successful mergers in real life. Consequently, the business world came up with an answer: creating synergies where the relationship is symbiotic and mutually beneficial. Such a relationship where the two companies benefit from each other's partnership is based on a resource-sharing concept, where respective economies of scale are used to generate greater profits for the involved companies.

An example of this symbiosis is the relationship between Amazon.com and Circuit City, where customers can order the products through the Amazon.com website and choose to either have the product delivered at home or choose to pick it up at the nearest Circuit City store. This pioneered the practice of in- store pick up, a concept that brings the e-tailers close to their brick and mortar counterparts.

While the relationship is truly symbiotic, businesses often succumb to the individual approach. February 2005 saw an end to this relationship. Circuit City announced that it will stop selling items through the Amazon.com website and focus on sales through its own website, which has shown promising results since it was revamped. Amazon.com started selling Circuit City products in 2001, and during the Thanksgiving sales of 2004 the company sold more electronic items than books for the first time.

Toys "R" Us is another company that chose to end this relationship with Amazon.com by filing a $200 million lawsuit against them for allowing third party vendors to sell products on its website. Amazon.com in turn filed a $750 million lawsuit against Toys "R" Us for failing to stock popular items. Court papers revealed that Toys "R" Us did not have adequate stocks of the most popular items about twenty percent of the time.

While many retailers continue to partner with Amazon.com, the stock market does not seem to penalize Amazon.com for the termination of these relationships. Having such alliances is crucial to the company as it continues to compete with improved and revamped websites of major traditional retailers such was Wal-Mart. The current website of the company is an improved version and very user friendly, offering high-ticket items from electronics to diamonds. Consistent with the Wal-Mart philosophy, the company continues to offer the lowest prices and very competitive shipping rates [3].

In addition to encouraging constructive innovation, the crash of the Internet dotcom bubble destroyed some prevalent beliefs, and this in turn has led to some constructive rather than imaginative innovation.

Primarily, the crash of the Internet bubble prevented companies from following the herd. Prior to the crash the idea was that the Internet changes everything. "E-everything" was considered the mantra to success. True, it changes the way we communicate, it changes how we access information, and it changes how we buy goods, but only for products that justify the additional cost involved in developing a marketplace platform.

Strictly for analytical purposes, let's take a look at Walmart.com, the online store of the retail industry leader. The company sells everything from low-ticket items to higher-end electronics. The website is useful only for items that justify the shipping costs. The low-ticket items come in handy when the consumer has to meet a particular dollar cutoff to take advantage of the free shipping offer. In other words, not every product sells successfully through the Internet. Typically, products that do not require the "feel and see" attribute for the consumer will sell well on the Internet. Think Amazon.com vs. Webvan [4].

Webvan is an online grocery company. The concept was ingenious; it catered to the needs of the elderly and busy professionals with time constraints. With a perfect name for its service, it lacked technology backup. Access to broadband connections was very limited in the years 2000 and 2001. The company received high customer satisfaction ratings; however, in addition to the fact that the company was expanding too rapidly what was missing was the technology upgrade at the consumer level. Grocery items accompanied by pictures that took too long to download cut into the ordering time, which gradually reduced the customer base. Though a pioneer in online grocery shopping, Webvan closed in July 2005.

Innovation is the spark behind technology, and a derivative of innovation is the principle of "first mover advantage." Many believed this to be the mantra to success during the 1990's. Examples such as Prodigy.net encouraged entrepreneurs to think otherwise. Briefly, the company was formed in 1984 as a joint venture between IBM, Sears and CBS, offering services such as news and communication through PCs. It was well ahead of its time. However, a series of operational mistakes, such as imposing a charge for sending e-mails beyond a certain number when competitors offered the service for free, finally led to its sale in 1996 to a group of investors. Certainly, Prodigy.net had the first mover advantage, and while first mover is important it is not necessarily the most important attribute of success.

Another widely held belief prior to the crash was that the customer is king. True, in this world of information overload the customer *is* king. That is, he is king insofar as he or she has access to price transparency and hence the power to make a more efficient decision with regard to best value for price. But the customer is not king with respect to price *negotiations*. Today, a consumer has the capability to research endless pages of data usually found on the Internet before deciding on subjects as varied as buying a new computer to undergoing major surgery. Information allows him to make a more educated decision, but all this does not give him the power to negotiate prices.

Economically speaking, the presence of the Internet does not make prices more elastic, it just increases the clarity in price comparison. In essence what we have here is a New Economy model that continues to stand on the foundation of Old Economy, but it is being built by new material and thoughts. Essentially the new business models are being promoted by creativity in the form of creating a unique company focus. What kinds of focus? It is the kind of focus that is synthesized in every decision the company takes, and it is the kind of focus that leads toward the business goals of the company and becomes central to the actions of every employee. However, the origination of that focus is critical.

Goals should foster and catalyze focus. This is another distinction between the successful and not-so-successful companies. "To attain a twenty-percent growth rate" or "To exceed market expectations by ten percent" are both examples of goals. Focus is essentially the philosophy that the company and its employees live within. It is a philosophy that is embedded in every aspect of the company's business model.

A good business model goes beyond the economics of generating revenues and reducing costs; it has a central focus that aligns behavior to business strategy. For the companies of today, this focus is very often the paradigm shift that allowed them to excel and change the rules. Business models define how a company will conduct its business and what will be the source of revenue.

Characteristics of revenue and cost-per–product are quite different. The revenue, or price, generated per product is the same if no volume discounts are offered, whereas the cost of a product decreases with every additional product sold. This is because as the company produces more the costs are distributed over a larger number; hence cost-per-product is less. There comes a point at which the company has sold enough products to cover its fixed costs: this is the "break-even point." Every additional product sold beyond the break-even point adds only a marginal cost for the company, and its revenue in excess of the marginal cost is what generates profit.

Profit is what every company strives for, and of course the higher the profit the better. This is where it gets competitive. An industry that shows immense potential for profit attracts competitors. As competitors increase, the possible resources available per company decrease because of crowding. It is true that over the gamut the leader will have the maximum market share, but the presence of multiple competitors reduces the return on investment. In economics this is called the law of diminishing returns, and this is essentially due to the crowding effect. The advent of technology challenges this and actually changes the law from diminishing marginal returns to increasing marginal returns. Additionally, sound business models identify the unique differentiators that prevent them from being copied.

Protection of business models under patent law is a much-debated topic. Patented or not, imitating the leading company's business model is extremely difficult, if not impossible. Why? Think about Dell, GE, Southwest Airlines, Wal-Mart and other similar companies. Business models of Dell, Wal-Mart, and Southwest Airlines have been researched and studied by many. GE pioneered the Six Sigma. Why is it that, in spite of knowing what these models are, no competitor has been able to duplicate the same success? The answer: because it is not their focus. They are imitating other companies. When companies try to duplicate a model they often fail because that focus is not instilled in every aspect of their business. It is not the central idea of every decision taken by every employee;

therefore, these behaviors do not translate to the same level of accomplishment. It is this unique differentiating element in their business models that causes the much-needed paradigm shift to succeed in this era of technology-enabled economy.

CHAPTER 6

Paradigm Shifters of the New Economy: They Started a Revolution

"Our remedies oft in ourselves do lie."

– William Shakespeare,
All's Well That Ends Well

CHAPTER 6

Unlike the Old Economy models that are organized by profit centers, the current business models are moving away from "profit centricity" to "customer centricity." The earlier strategy was to make a good product, and this creates a need for the product. But now the logic has been reversed. The New Economy trend is to listen to the needs of the consumer and then create a product. The driving force behind this is a more educated consumer. This is a consumer who has done his or her research and knows exactly what he or she wants. As economies across the globe improve, consumers from all walks of life are coming out with what they want to see in their favorite products. For instance, Proctor and Gamble observed the traditional mop's messy hazard of water slopping around and cleverly introduced the "Swiffer." This started a trend, and the term "Swiffering" became synonymous with "cleaning." Examples like this are mandating that companies switch their focus from numbers to customers.

Another aspect of the changing business model is the practice of off-shoring. While off-shoring is a recent phenomenon, outsourcing has been in existence in many forms within the USA for quite a while. Off-shoring basically moves American jobs to foreign countries for reduced labor costs. That, however, is only one side of the coin. The flipside is new avenues of growth within the US, and this growth comes from improved technologies and their applications. As customers demand more value per dollar spent, companies in all industries are forced to cut costs; hence, they look around for best value-for-dollar too, and off-shoring is one way to help them achieve this. Wal-Mart is often criticized for importing goods from China and India and not encouraging the production of locally made products, and unfortunately many companies are doing just that - and thereby reducing the number of their US employees and their wages. Opening the skies for developing countries is soon going to challenge the established models of the airline industry. The leading low-cost carrier, Southwest Airlines, could face serious competition from low-cost carriers from India. Jet Airways, the leading domestic carrier within India, serves a full, three-course meal in a typical forty-five-minute flight. Compare that with the bag of pretzels and a can of soda in a typical domestic two-hour flight in the US. Which airline would *you* prefer?

Another change within the successful business model is flexibility. The well-known phrase "the only thing constant is change" very aptly describes the new face of business. With information being distributed faster, consumers and investors alike have to react swiftly, mandating that companies react equally fast.

A recent *Wall Street Journal* article entitled "Wal-Mart's H-P Elves" [5] explains how Wal-Mart and H-P learned from the low holiday sales of 2004 to revamp their strategy for 2005. H-P designed special holiday laptops to be sold exclusively at Wal-Mart. The day after Thanksgiving, Wal-Mart was selling them for $388.00. Did either company make profits that went to the bottom line? Probably not. Instead, this promotion introduced Wal-Mart to a whole new section of the market - shoppers who typically bought computers and computer accessories at Best Buy or Circuit City. For H-P, the volume discounts they negotiated with their suppliers will enable lower costs in the future.

Another such recent change is in the business model of Starbucks Coffee. Starbucks recently started the drive-through option. Once again, the company listened to its customers by realizing the busy lifestyle of individuals, and it catered to the need by responding quickly and efficiently.

The above examples illuminate the growing importance of first listening to the consumer and then designing a product or service around it. "Assets are Employees and not Equipment" is the new paradigm. Human resources have always been the neglected aspect of the Old Economy. Actually, the company that understands this will automatically pay attention to the customer. The New Economy is changing this trend. The new trend is to recognize the "intellectual capital" of the labor force, and some companies are internally calling it an intangible asset.

Southwest Airlines is probably the best example for this. In times when most airlines have been struggling for profit and filing for bankruptcy, Southwest has emerged a winner. How did Southwest do this? For starters, it recognized that within all the factors important for airline travel the exclusivity of the staff uniform is probably the least important to the traveler. So it cut costs by making their uniform very simple. Southwest started hiring for the right person rather than the right approach. In the *Wall Street Journal* article "Keeping Ahead of the Pack," [6] Southwest Airlines CEO Gary Kelly states that he is not worried about competition. Even though his business model can be copied, what cannot be imitated are the people working in Southwest and the very culture of the company.

Another example is the case of the UPS union strike. Had FedEx employees not responded quickly and promptly, not only would the businesses have suffered but also the company would have lost the opportunity to capture a significant share of the market.

All employees believe in the company focus. Every action that they take is centered on the focus. The focus, whether low cost or technology, is instilled in the company atmosphere. This changing working environment is translating to a relaxed and more flexible working style for the employees, and in turn employers are receiving higher productivity.

A force behind this trend involves the change in how companies are being valued. Though not a part of mainstream valuations within the USA, companies in Europe are increasingly being valued at how they return and contribute to the society. In other words, what they are doing for the society from a social or philanthropic perspective matters. The trend has been labeled as corporate social responsibility. Websites such as www.csrnetwork.com and www.bitc.org.uk are examples of Europe's response to this trend. Consumers give preference to products not only from companies that are making a conscious effort to give back to the society but also to companies that are providing greater clarity to non-financial audits of a company operation.

With globalization and world trade barriers broken, it is only a matter of time before companies within North America and other parts of the world will be required to follow suit and provide clarity in recognizing and valuing the non-financial assets: their employees or their intellectual capital.

The Changing Marketing Scenario. With severe competition across the globe, businesses are looking for newer avenues to reach the consumer. In their search they have to invent better methods of communicating with their consumers. From consumers who come from countries as developed as the USA, to the consumers in the developing nations of the Asian region, and to those of the newly emerging economies of Europe all require efficient communication. In other words, standard box treatments don't work anymore. It's all about customization. When marketing trends need to be customized, understanding the consumer is key. And to do this companies need data. Gathering individual data is very expensive, so companies are open to sharing data with their suppliers and counterparts. Rather than competing secretly, they are now trying a more cooperative approach.

A classic example of understanding what the consumer needs can be found in the automotive industry. Unlike the US, personal cars - not just taxis and limousine-type cars - are also chauffer-driven in the Asian sub-continent of India. So if the same design would be implemented, the driver gets the five-axis seat control with all the best features, while the owner of the car, who occupies the rear seat, gets a simple forward backward manual control. Realizing this trend, the cars to be sold there had to be re-designed with this fact in mind.

Another aspect of the changing marketing scenario is the emergence of a creative economy. China took away the manufacturing jobs, and now India is doing the same to the service sector. So what happens to the US economy? To survive the US will need to reeducate its people, develop new creative economics, and increase the strength of its core intellectual capital. Companies are increasingly encouraging the in-house creativity of their employees. This will need to happen throughout the country with strong Government assistance and funding to transform our education system to meet this challenge.

Until recently companies have been concentrating on information processing. The trend has been to use past data and experiences as rules of thumb to develop future guidelines. These methods worked fine for the Old Economy, which was heavy on manufacturing and industrialization. However, the New Economy is dominated by factors such as continuously changing technology, synergies across the value chain, and increased free trade across geographical borders. All of these trends demand a very high amount of flexibility both in thinking and acting.

Further, old world belief has been to collect and store data. But this data is static. This approach is being replaced by renewal of existing knowledge and creation of new knowledge.

As the global business environment demands more cooperation, companies are finding new ways to understand their consumers. Amazon's use of collaborative-filtering, Wal-Mart's supply chain management, and Dell's logistics are examples of how the marketing scenarios have and will continue to change.

Recognizing Business Intelligence. Intelligence is traditionally related to solving mathematical or scientific dilemmas. But thinkers such as Howard Gardner of Harvard University have identified intelligence in different forms. Mozart, gifted football players, and artists are all intelligent in their respective fields. Could it be that the knack to do business is also in-born? Could it be that some of us just have a better sense of recognizing the emerging and future trends before others? Daniel P. Goleman has discussed the idea at length within the introduction of the book *Business: The Ultimate Resource* [7]. This aspect is indirectly, if not directly, changing the role of management. The old world economy had standard hierarchy and work flow guidelines. The New Economy requires all involved to be flexible: the employees, the management, and the company as a whole. Management's role is no longer to control but constantly to search, to sense, to recognize and to respond to the emerging trends. This paradigm shift is the key to success.

Human beings by nature need structure and guidelines to work. Even though new ideas may come from employees or customers, the task of sensing them as future trends is management responsibility. Consequently, management has to train itself and its employees to expect surprises and not predictability in their respective business environments.

The Enabler: Technology. Paul Roemer very precisely described the whole concept of the New Economy and technology when he said in *The Wall Street Journal* in May 1999, "It isn't so much that we have a New Economy as we have a new understanding of the importance of technology in the New Economy." As discussed earlier, the word technology means different things to different individuals. For the 21st century, technology has become synonymous with the electronics industry. When a common person talks about technological advances, he is talking about advances in the PC industry, advanced features in Palm Pilots, cell phones, and the like. This is, in fact, a very narrow view of this expanding industry and the future convergence between very different technologies. For example, hardware, telephony, PC, applications, networks, and even whole industries are merging. Consider the new I-Phone from Apple Computer which was recently announced. A PC company is now in the telecommunications industry and partnering with a service provider.

Technological advances have sprung up in the most amazing places. The simplest technological breakthroughs are often overlooked under the awe and aura of the bigger innovations. Take a look at the company 3M. From a consumer perspective the company has probably given one of the most useful products for the office supply industry – scotch tape [8] . But how often does one consider scotch tape to be a technological breakthrough? In other words, "technology" is about application of knowledge to create a product that increases productivity, not only about microchips.

For the New Economy technology is central. And here, in addition to being the common enabler for all paradigms, technology is also synonymous with advances in industries either directly or tangentially related to electronics.

The Spill Over effect has had multiple repercussions, and advances in technology have changed the economic theory of diminishing returns and introduced the new era economics of increasing returns. This has forced organizations to look beyond their immediate competition and find opportunities for creating synergies across their respective value chains. The Internet alone has not changed how companies do business, but it has opened windows of opportunity. This can be likened to what happened when Edison captured electricity, metaphorically speaking, to bring us out of the darkness into light. In return, a revolution happened. The very act of harnessing electricity in small bulbs allowed inventors to use it in novel ways. Without electricity there would have been no cars, no radios, no computers, and more importantly, no technology as we know it today.

As the importance of technology and its application increased, the effects could also be observed in the stock market. During the 1970's the manufacturing industries dominated the market, and by the 1990's manufacturing had been replaced by high tech. Once again, the word high-tech had a range of implications. For those who understood its true meaning, companies were created that have redefined whole businesses; and for those who just wanted to join the bandwagon, it was a possible source of making a quick fortune. Unfortunately, the quick fortune led to great losses with the stock market crash.

How did technology enable companies to capitalize on their unique focus? The single biggest contributor towards technology implementation has been proprietary thinking, be it in the form of Google's unique search algorithm or Amazon's answer to collaborative filtering.

The interesting point here is that these companies have not tried to re-invent the wheel in any situation. They have only made it better. Google learned from AOL and Yahoo to improve upon the spider technology and arrive at their ranking system. Amazon.com used the concept of collaborative filtering and took it a step further by bundling it with other products that are often complementary to the main purchase.

Southwest Airlines, on the other hand, used principles of academic human resources and applied them to their business model. This worked well for them because the airline industry depends upon good customer service. Hence, it only made sense to develop a business model that was people-centric. Again, that is people-centric, not consumer-centric. The cause of success for people-centric models is the company's own employees, just as in the case of Southwest Airlines. For Southwest, the technology was not in any software but in redefining the process to change some standard industry rules, such as having no specific seat assignments and allowing point-to-point travel. Even more important was the paradigm shift in their choice of competition. Unlike the legacy carriers who chose to compete against each other, Southwest chose to compete against the alternative to air-transportation: car travel.

Apple and Dell are two companies that changed the fate of the PC industry and used technology in very different ways. For Apple, technology implied simplifying high tech innovation and bringing it down to a machine that would basically guide a user on how to use it. This is exactly what Apple did by introducing the interactive Graphic User Interface and the mouse. It eliminated the common image of a computer as a fearsome object surrounded by wires and replaced it with a sleek machine in fashion-conscious colors that were bold enough to accentuate an interior.

For Dell, technology has been geared towards improving upon their logistics and supply chain and finessing it to a point where the computer manufacturer does not have any raw material inventory. This is a feat that has not been repeated by any other company within the industry with equal success.

Thus, we see that while the common man associates technology with high-tech gadgets, in the actual world of business technology implementation incorporates a wider spectrum.

CHAPTER 7

Companies: Changing the Rules of the Game

"Now is the winter of our discontent."

– William Shakespeare,
Richard III

CHAPTER 7

SEARCH ENGINE INDUSTRY

Ask anyone to define the Internet and the response in most cases would be close to "it's a tool to communicate, access, and share a vast pool of knowledge." Few realize the technical definition of the Internet in its simplest form surrounds a network of computers that operates using a standardized communication protocol. Its origin dates back to 1969 when four interconnected computers, called the ARPANET [9], were used to share information across the Defense Department.

An important tool for the flow of information across the globe through millions of connected computers is the search engine. A search engine facilitates finding information on the World Wide Web (WWW) through the Internet. Search engine software consists of a server or a collection of servers dedicated to indexing Internet web pages, storing the results, and returning lists of pages to match user queries.

As the information available on the WWW began to expand, accurately and efficiently locating information was restricted to the literate few who knew how to find it. It was sometime in 1994 when two Stanford Ph.D. students, David Filo and Jerry Yang, created a list of their favorites by organizing them in different categories on their personal web page. Little did they know that this simple directory of theirs would change how the world communicates, finds, and accesses information. What was once known as "David and Jerry's Guide to the World Wide Web" is now the popular "Yahoo, Inc."

Yahoo. We now know that Yahoo's origin was simply a directory created by its founders for their own personal use. The usefulness of such a tool started to spread through word of mouth, and in just five short months "David and Jerry's Guide to the World Wide Web" was accessed by 100,000 online users. With such a positive response to their directory, the founders knew they had a business idea with great potential on hand. This led to Yahoo's incorporation in March 1995.

Prior to Yahoo in the early 1990s, the search engine methodology included primarily spider-based engines such as AltaVista.com, whereas Yahoo introduced the concept of "directories." With information organized in directories, and instead of using key word searches for the WWW, one can search information specific to a particular topic. Gaining popularity, Yahoo launched a successful IPO in 1996. Along with going public comes the responsibility of making sufficient profit to justify a company's market capitalization and to meet the market expectation quarter after quarter.

The IPO gave Yahoo the impetus it needed to look beyond the technical innovation and into the business side of the company. This started the era of acquisitions, with the most recent one being Pixoria and Flickr.com, making Yahoo, Inc. one of the most comprehensive horizontal portals on the web [10].

How did Yahoo survive the stock market crash? Yahoo, Inc. took advantage of the first mover advantage, and this one step also became the key differentiator for Yahoo, Inc. establishing itself on the WWW. The First Mover Advantage can be defined as "the benefit firms can reap by being first in their industry." Yahoo was not the first search engine to enter the industry, but it took leadership to organize the vast amount of information in directories. Yahoo helped to categorize the information, making it more user-friendly.

When understanding this, it is important to remember that computer literacy and Internet savvy was very limited in the 1990's. In fact, not everyone owned a computer. Libraries offered beginner courses teaching basics such as "How to Browse the World Wide Web." In time Yahoo gave its users the option of making Yahoo.com the computer owner's homepage. Instead of thinking of keywords to search, the website allowed its users to simply click on key directories such as "finance" and "education" and search within the sub-directories to access information. This took away a considerable amount of thinking from the user's hands to the hands of Yahoo, Inc., where the information was categorized.

Subsequent to the partial recession of the early 90's, the second half of the last decade in the 20th century was also the era in which business models have been redefined. It is often said that "Necessity is the mother of invention." The timing of the slow economy and the advent of the Internet may be coincidental, but it is the slowing growth that created the necessity to boost profits and to look for avenues to do so. The individuals who had the business savvy and the courage to look beyond the present took risks and gave birth to the e-giants of today. Besides Yahoo Inc., other examples include Amazon.com, Google.com, and Monster.com. Unknowingly, these companies gave each other the media publicity boost that they needed.

The introduction of unconventional business ideas was needed both by the businesses and the consumers. The businesses needed that new avenue to explore profit-making opportunities; the consumers needed a signal of an improving economy. The combined effect of all these events gave Yahoo, Inc., and other Internet companies the media publicity they needed, hence directing traffic to their sites and boosting their market potential.

It would be unfair to state that pure luck and coincidence contributed to Yahoo's success. While being the first did play a major role, a second differentiating factor is its management's business intelligence to recognize and understand consumer needs and how to integrate them into its business model. Free e-mail, web pages, games, and financial information were added to Yahoo's website as added value to the consumer, but they also ensured that consumers came back to Yahoo's website.

Over time, as Yahoo established itself as a one-stop portal for accessing information ranging from financial stock quotes to price comparison, at no cost to the consumer, the company then decided to change their business model from free services to a cost to consumers.

This is the major turn in Yahoo's history. Why? This one decision took Yahoo from being an organized (categorized) tool used to search information on the net to one of the most popular commercial web portals. In fact, the directories, which were the highlight of its homepage in the earlier years, are now at the bottom of the page. Even when clicked on, the directory appears as a side bar to the other information. This change in the design of its homepage signaled a major shift in the company's focus.

While this change has allowed Yahoo to increase revenues, it has also allowed competition to edge in and gain leadership. The competition is the mega company called Google, Inc.

Google. While Yahoo was gaining momentum and popularity through both its increased usage and IPO in 1996, two other Stanford PhD students, Larry Page and Sergey Brin, were laying the foundations for yet another Internet phenomenon. The two students were working on a search engine project called "Back Rub." The name highlights the engine's unique capability to analyze the back links to a website.

The previous models of search engines such as Excite.com and AltaVista.com provided results based on assessing the number of links *from* a given website, whereas Google rankings are based on links *to* a given website. Author John Battelle, in his book *The Search*, very perceptively compares this to the system used in the field of academics. Research on any topic often has various citations, and the more citations to a particular paper the more influential that paper becomes. Translating this to the search engine, the more often users link to a website the higher that site's ranking. The higher a site's ranking the better its chances of being found and linked to again. This out-of-the-box thinking, combined with a rather academic or technical approach to the challenge, enabled Google to distinguish itself from the crowd.

Yahoo's presence and immense success had taken away the first mover advantage from Google. Instead of reinventing the search engine model or the evolving web portal model, Google's success depended on improving upon the existing technology.

A US Department of Commerce study on the digital divide, "Falling through the Net - Defining the Digital Divide," indicates a small increase of just eighteen percent over a period of four years in the number of households that had a computer at home. Though small, this percentage signifies something important: the late majority and the laggards within the consumer segment were now coming out of their shells and investing in computers. Consequently, by 1998 the Internet usage within the professional arena was within the range of forty-five to sixty percent. At this point it is important to mention that the digital divide between the rural and central

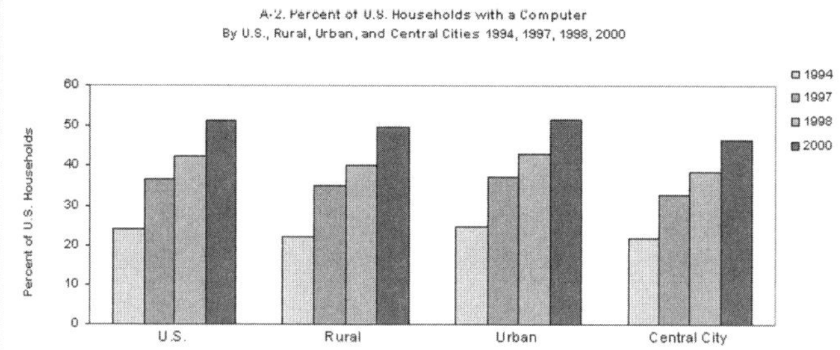

	U.S.	Rural	Urban	Central City
1994	24.1	22.1	24.8	22.0
1997	36.6	34.9	37.2	32.8
1998	42.1	39.9	42.9	38.5
2000	51.0	49.6	51.5	46.3

Source: NTIA and ESA, U.S. Department of Commerce, using U.S. Bureau of the Census Current Population Survey supplements.

city areas was one of the biggest concerns of both lawmakers and the professional world. For the lawmakers it signaled an increasing disparity among the work force and salary structure. For the business community the existence of the digital divide meant an untapped consumer base.

What did this do for Google? It did nothing, really, other than signify the growing importance of computers. This increased importance of computers had started a ripple effect for Internet usage, the e-era for businesses, and for changing the laws to accommodate the uniqueness of this technology. Ironically, in some ways all this concern for the growing digital divide, lack of computers in schools, and many similar social issues probably laid the foundation for the success of many Internet-based ventures.

Yahoo's popularity and its catchy advertising phrase, "Do you Yahoo?," combined with the media publicity and the increasing returns in IT investments, had sparked an interest in many other e-companies. This created an easy entry for Google. Once again, like Yahoo, word-of-mouth followed by media popularity is what spread the advertising message around for Google, Inc. A key difference between Yahoo and Google technology is that Google needs keyword search. So, with the first mover advantage credited to Yahoo and the increased mandatory requirement of being net-savvy from a consumer perspective, how did Google take the lead? The answer is simple: culture. Google, Inc. is probably one of the few companies where the inherent working culture was centered on technology.

In comparison, Yahoo started off as a hobby that evolved into a business, whereas Google started off as a research project to understand the anatomy of the search engines and make them better. This has continued to be the focus of the company. And, in turn, the core of the company culture is staying true to its focus and not getting bogged down by market expectations and the business side. The focus for Google is still technology.

Yahoo is a web portal that integrates different technologies sourced through acquisitions. Microsoft, another major competitor for Google, is a software company. Google is not an integrator; rather it is both a software and hardware company.

The most important factor for focus on technology is the fact that founders Page and Brin continue to hold a major stake in the company. As stated on the company website, Larry Page is the President over Products, and Sergey Brin is President over Technology. Contrast this to information on the Yahoo website, where the co-founders Filo and Yang are designated as Chief Yahoo and Director respectively, suggesting a less involved role in the technical process. The involved behavior of the respective founders is also echoed in the company information presented on the websites. Despite being recognized as the search engine of choice by many, the founders of Google acknowledge that it is not perfect because a perfect search engine would know exactly what its users want.

Although Google was not a first mover in search engines, they did pioneer the first wireless technology for mobile communication. Currently, Google provides its wireless technology to numerous market leaders including AT&T Wireless, Sprint PCS, and Palm, among others. Like all start up companies, founders Page and Brin were short on cash; and rather than accepting the norms of the industry and finding financial help, they decided to look for alternate solutions for faster connectivity within their budget. Their innovation of linking PC's to find each query's answer quickly paid off in faster response times, greater scalability, and lower costs. This innovative attitude and out-of-the-box thinking has also carried forward to its business model.

When the company decided to go public, it did not choose the standard IPO process but rather the unconventional way of having an open IPO. Why did the company choose to do so? There are different theories surrounding this, and they are all correct from their own perspectives. But the single biggest advantage of choosing the open IPO was that the company, in addition to being innovative, did not lose sight of its second focus: the customer. By looking to the process of how an open IPO works, the single biggest winner is the customer or consumer. For Google, these customers are also the end users. By providing them a comparable, if not an equal, access to its shares, Google stayed true to its focus of being customer-centric. Customer-centricity is echoed throughout the company's website both by simple interface and by its list of objectives.

However, the current competitive scenario for Google, Inc. has been changing very rapidly. With all the attention on Google, investors had forgotten Yahoo for a while, but recent debates and possible legal battles for Google regarding consumer privacy and its effort to digitize copyright material have raised concerns about the future of the company. While industry analysts do agree that there is room for both companies in the search engine industry, it is also acknowledged by many that the gap between the two is diminishing. Though numerically the difference between Yahoo and Google is still large, caution is resurfacing, and memories of the Internet crash are beginning to emerge in the minds of the investing communities. At the end of the day, it all comes down to a battle between Yahoo's strategy of acquisitions versus Google's strong belief in encouraging internal innovation through its unique working culture.

It is true that Google and Yahoo have changed the process of accessing or searching information on the Internet. However, the foundation for this was laid almost a decade before these companies were founded. The foundation was laid when Steve Case formed Quantum Computer Services in 1985. In 1989 this company acquired a new name - America Online, or AOL for short.

AOL. The target market for the company was the computer illiterate, in contrast to its competition, CompuServe, which required technical ability and skills to use the system. The company catered to this by introducing key word search instead of requiring the www.companyname.com format. This allowed users to search for a particular company simply by typing in the keyword. AOL also catered to human interaction by catch phrases such as, "You've got mail," which played a very important role in its advertising campaign to gain market share. Another opportunity for human interaction was created through chat rooms, where like-minded people could exchange information.

The initial fee structure of the company was based on hours of usage, but in 1996, with increased competition in the industry, the company changed to a flat fee of $19.99 per month. While the distinguishing feature for the company was its ability to cater to people unfamiliar with computers, the cause of its demise was success. The company gained immense popularity and criticism at the same time. An increasing customer base resulted in busy signals for many that led to cancellation of accounts. The AOL software was notorious for blocking its users from using any other ISP (Internet Service Provider). As a result, in 2000 the company faced an $8 billion dollar class action lawsuit [11] .

Additionally, AOL's marketing strategy was annoying consumers. The company sent out software discs with special promotions; the promotion continues to receive backlash from environmentalists and other active groups stating the CDs are a source of non-biodegradable material and unsolicited advertising.

The AOL-Time Warner merger was the mega-merger that created waves. The masterminds behind the merger called it "a merger of bringing additional value to the consumer," and when the merger happened, Wall Street decided to knock down $30 billion. The two men behind it, Steve Case and Gerald Levin, presented their thoughts on why they thought the merger meant additional value for the consumers in an interview with Jim Lehrer [12] . Essentially, what the men imagined was the capability to use the television for some of the tasks performed by a PC. For example, while watching a TV show you decide to send an e-mail to someone who might be interested in it. And the technologies of the two companies combined would allow the consumer to do that. It's now 2007. Has this happened?

Jim Lehrer, the interviewer, rightfully asked the gentlemen, "Are you sure that the consumers want to do this, or is this a decision you all have made and you want to sell it to them?" This was the vital question that was probably not answered in any of the pre-merger meetings. Did consumers want this? How would the consumers view the merger? From a layman's perspective, this merger was an attempt to gain on the Internet boom. Time Warner was the leader in the media industry. AOL, at that point, still had popularity as an ISP and commanded a leading authority. Remember, AOL was an ISP, whereas Yahoo and Google were search engines. So, while the promises made at the time of the merger were big, the actual realization of those promises has been very disappointing.

This is probably best illustrated by the company's stock performance. At the beginning of 2000 Time Warner stock (TWX) was trading at a high of approximately $83.38 and a low of $74.75. However, by the end of the year 2000 (the year of merger) the stock price had dropped to a low of $35.35, a drop of greater than one-half. Why was the market not rewarding the company for the synergies created through the mega merger?

Both prior and subsequent to the merger, the company's growth is credited to a stream of acquisitions. The list of acquired companies include competitors CompuServe, Mirabilis Ltd. (ICQ Technology), Netscape, Mapquest, Inc., and the most recent ones being the Internet video search Truveo and the digital music subscription company MusicNow. Though the company pioneered the industry in creating a platform that eliminated the computer literacy barrier, it lost the leading position by moving away from its focus because, in some ways, it did not have a focus. If its focus was to cater to people unfamiliar with computers, it should have continued to do so. Now, computer literacy has increased; however, even today there are many aspects of the Internet that an average user is unfamiliar with.

The recent worries of the Time Warner breakup are a further signal of how synergies on paper do not necessarily translate to practical synergies. Though in certain ways AOL is ancestral to Yahoo and Google, it does not occupy a position before them because, unlike its predecessors that continue to have a focus, AOL will need to redefine and find that focus once again to re-establish its leadership in the competitive market of Internet service providers and search engines.

Internet providers and search engines go hand in hand, but how do industries dominated by traditional brick-and-mortar business models translate or compete within the new e-economy? It is important to understand the transition of brick-and-mortar to the virtual model in relation to the retailing industry.

RETAILING TO E-RETAILING (E-TAIL INDUSTRY):

Any discussion about the retail industry cannot be complete without the mention of the one company that changed the very essence of high profit margins. The retailing industry essentially has either niche sales or mass sales. Within the mass sales, the profit margins are still considerably high. Discount retailing was often associated with inferior quality products. But one company changed it all, and they changed it in a way that, despite opposition, competition was forced to follow.

Fred Smith, founder and CEO of FedEx, was asked in an interview with USA TODAY's corporate management reporter Del Jones: "If there was a Mount Rushmore of CEOs, whose face would be on it?"

His answer included many famous names including: "Alfred Sloan of General Motors. (Henry) Ford owned the auto industry, but he recognized that the country was becoming more affluent and marketing was becoming more important. Tom Watson Jr. at IBM made the courageous decision down the path into computing and modern mainframe computers." He added, "Probably (William) Allen of Boeing. He bet on the swept-wing jet that led his company's aerospace dominance for many years. How could you not put (Wal-Mart's) Sam Walton there? He allowed people of modest incomes to have a standard of living they never thought of." [13]

In addition to identifying Sam Walton as one of the legendary figures that changed the face of American industry, Fred Smith has, in this one sentence, very simply but very effectively described what Wal-Mart has given to America; and it is now spreading that same philosophy across the globe. 1962 was the year of discount retailing when Wal-Mart, Kmart, and Target opened doors. Wal-Mart founder Sam Walton started the company with a single focus: low cost. After establishing this focus, everything the company did was centered on the low-cost philosophy.

Wal-Mart. Wal-Mart is often criticized for importing foreign products to the US, and hence decreasing the demand for domestic products. While that is one side of the coin, some economists argue that as economies open, markets become more efficient, and products with best value for the money flow across national boundaries. When such a trend happens, the winner almost always is the consumer. At least in the short term. However, over the longer term this apparent benefit also needs to take into account the consequences for the local economy and employment conditions for local employees.

To understand the success of Wal-Mart it is important to understand the driving force: its founder, Sam Walton. Sam Walton's vision is simply stated: "The secret of successful retailing is to give your customers what they want. And really, if you think about it from your point of view as a customer, you want everything: a wide assortment of good-quality merchandise; the lowest possible prices; guaranteed satisfaction with what you buy; friendly, knowledgeable service; convenient hours; free parking; a pleasant shopping experience."[14] Sam Walton's biggest strength was he was not afraid of innovation. This, combined with the vision to give his customers the lowest possible price, has created an unbeatable empire.

As he started his company in Bentonville, Arkansas, he realized the importance of channeling goods and streamlining the flow of information from the stores to the merchandise distribution houses. With this objective and the low-cost focus, the company decided to invest in technology to make this happen. When and how should the suppliers ship their products so that Wal-Mart stores can always have the popular items in stock? The logical answer is, only when the suppliers know to do so. Prior to Wal-Mart's redesigning of the supply chain logistics, supplying was based on specific order requests from vendors; there was no real-time data available for the suppliers to see which items are selling faster and where. Wal-Mart decided to change it and make their suppliers partners to success.

Wal-Mart achieved this by sharing sales data and re-designing logistics. Wal-Mart cash registers are connected live to their distribution centers, so every time the cashier rings up a product the corresponding distribution center makes note of it and notifies the supplier when to replenish a store. Wal-Mart digitized the supply chain and logistics at its distribution centers to such accuracy that products flow continuously with a window of twenty minutes from start to finish.

This accuracy did two things. First, suppliers had real time data that allowed them to make a better judgment on whether their products had any regional preferences. Second, by sharing data with the suppliers Wal-Mart made it mandatory for them to upgrade their technology. Most suppliers have done so. Procter and Gamble, for example, has a 200 person workforce stationed at Bentonville, Arkansas, working exclusively for one client – Wal-Mart.[15]

So why don't Target and other discount retailers follow suit? The answer: after studying the leader, the competition does realize the answer; however, the execution of the plan makes the difference. Target, for example, is achieving this with its Amazon.com alliance. Amazon.com has achieved the same efficiency in the market-space that Wal-Mart has achieved in the marketplace. By using the technology platform of Amazon.com, Target is receiving the benefits of harnessing technology to improve customer loyalty.

Having a distinct focal point differentiated Wal-Mart from its competitor. Wal-Mart has been and continues to be an example of the fact that costs of installing state-of-the-art technology do not necessarily mean higher prices for its consumers. Now, after achieving success in the traditional brick-and-mortar stores, Wal-Mart continues the challenge by re-vamping its website and posing a threat to its counterparts, such as Amazon.com. Though appearing to be simple, the path from conventional brick-and-mortar stores to virtual marketplaces has been a continuously evolving technological challenge.

Retailing in its simplest form can be defined as the process of selling items to individual consumers. The venue of sale could be a large super center or a small family-run neighborhood store. The business model not only caters to the human need of actually feeling and examining the product before purchase, but it also provides instant gratification to the consumer. While retailer credibility is built from word of mouth and consumer experiences, that which defines the initial success for a company engaged in the business of retailing is location. It's all about location. Finding that ideal piece of land that meets the zoning criteria and yet is central and en route to its customers is critical. These unique attributes are also challenges faced by the retailing industry.

Add to it the challenge of doing all of this on the Internet and we have the next level of consumer shopping: E-Retailing, or the E-tail industry. If traditional stores are about location, the E-tail industry is all about technology. Technology enables the use of credit cards in a secure environment; it also enables the supply chain and the procurement process from placing an order to shipping it. Complex algorithms can solve the above challenges, but how does one solve the challenge of digitizing emotions and convincing a consumer to make a purchase without actually examining the product and, even more importantly, paying before use? The answer is hidden on the company website. The website is to the e-world what a business card is for the brick world. The website is the entrance for the virtual marketplace; hence, creating a window display that is not only eye-catching but also extremely user-friendly is fundamental to a company's success.

THE PROCESS OF PURCHASING A PRODUCT ONLINE

FROM THE SELLER'S PERSPECTIVE	FROM THE CONSUMER'S PERSPECTIVE
Guide the consumer to its website.	Identify the product that satisfies their need.
Help the consumer find the right product.	Compare prices.
A user-friendly experience – to discourage shopping around.	Identify the seller – providing the best value for money.
Offer reliable and cost effective shipping rates.	Verify reliability of seller.
State "return policy" clearly and precisely.	Place order by making payment.
Provide a human customer service number.	Await shipment.

The table above is an attempt to itemize the steps involved from both the seller's and the buyer's perspectives. This difference highlights two important issues. First, for the e-tail industry, the consumers have multiple research and buying options, including the option of researching online and purchasing offline. The second difference, and probably a more important one from the company perspective, is that all the steps involved center around the company website. Designing a website that not only encourages consumers to browse further beyond their needs but also helps consumers find products, and entices them to look at other complementary products, is fundamental for an e-tail business to succeed.

The year 1995 will go down in history as the year of birth for online shopping. That year saw the beginning of two e-tail companies: Amazon.com and eBay, Inc. Ten years after the advent of online shopping, consumers are shopping online in ever-increasing numbers. As of today, experts state that about six percent of total retail [16] sales in the US are online, while the offline sales are being heavily influenced by the online research conducted by consumers. The credit for this increasing trend of online shopping can be rightfully given to one company that changed the scene for retailers: Amazon.com.

Amazon.com: The Beginning of Online Shopping. Development of Amazon.com could not have been an easy process. The unique traits of the retail industry are twice as difficult to duplicate in a virtual world. Digitizing emotions and making a purchase without instant gratification for the consumer do not transfer over the Internet. For the seller, instant gratification and a source of revenue offset the costs before shipping the item. Add to the above the competitive industry environment both within and outside of the Internet and the challenge of implementing a successful business model gets even more difficult.

CHAPTER 7

So how did Amazon.com survive the Internet crash [17] and emerge a winner? Based in Seattle, Washington, and the brainchild of CEO Jeff Bezos, the company took roots when Bezos came across a statistic that the Internet was growing at an exponential rate of 2,300%. His combined skills and experience in the field of technology and finance logically and correctly led him to believe that such growth and potential signaled an emerging trend. The Internet would go beyond being a tool for communication and accessing information between different users. Based on this reasoning he identified twenty classes of items that could be sold over a remote medium like the Internet and then narrowed the list to two: books and music. He finally chose books, primarily because there are many more titles to sell with less restrictive guidelines from publishing houses when compared to music companies. Furthermore, market data indicated that the largest competitor, Barnes and Noble, had only twelve percent of the total volume of sales. And last, the very nature of the item made the product easy to ship.

One might ask, why Seattle? Why not locate the headquarters in the central part of the country for access to easy distribution? Once again, Bezos' natural business sense came into play. Seattle had no state income tax, it was close to a major publishing house (Ingram's Warehouse), and there was a wealth of talent in the immediate area. All these factors combined to make Seattle his preferred choice.

Even though the business plan of Amazon.com did not project profits for the initial years, the plan's success was established in its very first month when the company shipped books to all fifty states and to forty-five countries. While it is true that Amazon.com would not have achieved success had it not been for technology, the differentiating factor can easily be identified as the business intelligence of founder Jeff Bezos.

What is business intelligence? In the introduction to his book, *Business: The Ultimate Resource*, David P. Goleman defines business intelligence as "the capability to solve problems and challenges." In the same book Goleman raises the question:

> *"Just as we have IQ and EQ, can there be 'business intelligence?' A set of essential capabilities to succeed in the marketplace? To handle challenges in a way that not only offers a solution but also adds value? The capability to look beyond the immediate horizon and identify an emerging trend and capitalize on it? Could it be that some of us are just born with it?"*

Business intelligence has been evident in every stage of building Amazon.com. Bezos recognized a trend because the increased usage of Internet was a well-known fact. But his ability to look beyond the numbers and to identify the Internet as a tool for trade and communication, plus the seemingly simple identification of books as the first product, was revolutionary.

The company acted promptly. During the early 1990's many were talking about the potential of the Internet; however, only a few took action to utilize and increase its potential. One could say that Amazon.com also had the first mover advantage. True, it did; however, this advantage would not have done much had it not been for the innovation that led to the success of the company.

Innovation is a natural byproduct of business intelligence. And in all of this, technology is the enabler. Innovation and technology are intertwined in Amazon.com. Prior to developing any technology, the company established some basic principles:

- To be the "earth's most customer-centric company."

- To be identified as an Internet company and not as a competitor for its brick counterparts.

- To achieve this by sending the right signals to the market.

- To give the company the name "Amazon.com" and not "Amazon."

These evolved into new uses of technology - for example, to have Amazon provide products that "identify" potential consumers' requirements based on past buying preferences.

The significance of the name was not held internally; Bezos made sure that both the media and consumers understood the significance of this name through its press release. "Amazon.com's name pays homage to the Amazon River. Just as the Amazon River is Earth's biggest river--Amazon.com is Earth's Biggest Bookstore, offering 14 times the number of titles carried by the largest physical book superstore." [18] The "dot.com" extension conveys clearly that it is an Internet-based company and not a storefront for a traditional retailer. Consider this in relation to the fact that Internet awareness was not as widespread when Amazon.com started operations; this was a very important aspect for the company to position itself correctly in the competitive market.

In continuation of reinforcing the company's focus, customer-centric Amazon.com improved its website and tried to capture the same experiences a consumer looks for in traditional shopping. By doing this, Amazon.com allowed its consumers to transition easily from traditional bookstores to online purchases. Icons such as "shopping cart," "proceed to checkout," "one-click purchase," and "your store," prompt responses to purchase order inquiries, and reasonable delivery rates and estimates are all efforts that eased initial consumer fears about purchasing items online. These seemingly insignificant details not only enhanced customers' comfort in buying, they also sharply reduced customer resistance toward returning for other purchases.

Collaborative filtering is well known in marketing. It involves producing personal recommendations by comparing preferences between an individual and a group (sample) of people. Executing this task manually is quite challenging. Amazon.com used technology to perform this task. Staying true to its customer-centric focus, Amazon.com created a model in which products find consumers instead of consumers finding products. The ideas of bundled products and website recommendations are classic examples of products finding buyers without an initial search. Another feature, "Our recommendations for you …," is also based on an individual's purchase history that encourages more browsing and purchasing from the company. [19]

Once Amazon.com had established itself with its first product (books) the company decided it was time to move on to other products, so it created synergies across the value chain by strategic alliances with companies such as Toys "R" Us and Circuit City. The Amazon.com contracts with both of these companies have since ended, but while they were in force they helped to broaden Amazon.com's product offering.

As Amazon.com evolves into a portal rather than a retailer solely for books, both differences between sellers and price wars are evident - especially since Amazon.com has its own version of eBay in the form of zShops that allows third parties to showcase their products.

However, this does not undermine its capability to continue to be a leader in online shopping; it is co-opetition at its best. We say co-opetition and not competition because, despite recent downturns in some of its contracts, Amazon.com continues to provide healthy competition to both its online and offline competitors. Even with Circuit City, the mandate was not to ship through Amazon.com; the customers could pick up their purchases at a store. This is healthy competition.

With great economies of scale and technology as the single biggest asset already in place, the company could introduce new products with the same software and use its existing customer base to market those products. A quick look at Amazon.com's net value reveals that both the complementary and supplementary products to the company's product line are also a strong source of competition. For example, a complementary product to music CD's is CD players found at Best Buy or Circuit City, while supplementary sources are Borders and Wal-Mart. To compete with these businesses, rather than price cutting them, what did Amazon.com do? It created synergies. In 2001 Amazon.com created synergy with Target and Circuit City and offered them a platform to sell their products through Amazon.com. For the company it eliminated competition, whereas the opportunity gave the stores an established channel for distribution without incurring the additional investment costs.

Opponents of Amazon.com may state that it was the pure hype created by its founder, Jeff Bezos, which led to the success of Amazon.com. However, his business intelligence realized that when cash is in shortage, as it is with most startups, self-hype is the least expensive way to advertise your company. Combining his technology background with his business acumen, and realizing that the Web belongs to the users and not a particular company, Bezos successfully changed a few paradigms in the world of e-Retailing, with the most prominent one being redefining customer-centricity.

While Amazon.com was creating history and redefining the shopping experience for consumers, another company, eBay,

Inc., (eBay), was creating news by catering to another facet of the human shopping experience: the thrill of finding unique items at prices consumers could afford. Flea markets in the Old Economy sold everything from valuable antiques to items that were basically outdated or not needed in households; eBay is the New Economy equivalent of the flea market.

eBay. It is well known that Pierre Omidyar [20] founded eBay on Labor Day of 1995. The company facilitates the sale of goods from one person to another. It acts like a meeting place for buyers and sellers. Just as in its offline counterpart of actual flea markets where vendors develop a reputation for service, price, and credibility, sellers (vendors) participating on eBay develop a rating based on customer feedback. As their ratings and reviews improve, they establish a credibility record on the website.

While eBay started off as a platform or marketplace to trade collectibles and hard-to-find items, the company has now evolved into a market for a much wider range of items ranging from small trinkets like costume jewelry to used cars. For the year 2005 the company reported a consolidated net revenue stream of $4.55 billion, amounting to a thirty-nine percent increase over its previous year's figure of $3.27 billion. Forbes identified the eBay model as the "Best Business Model" on the Internet. [21]

The eBay business model is multi-faceted. As a company, eBay does not carry any inventory. The single biggest asset and expenditure for eBay is its technology. The company charges a non-refundable fee for listing an item for sale, called an insertion fee, and it takes a percentage commission based on the final bid price of the item. Opponents claim that the business model can be easily duplicated. Maybe, but what cannot be duplicated is the brand value, name recognition, and the consumer trust this website has attained. Close to the end of the third quarter, eBay reported 168 million registered users worldwide. The earth's population is estimated to be approximately 6.4 billion. [22] That means almost three percent of the earth's population shops with eBay as either a buyer or a seller. This in itself is quite an amazing achievement.

Though founded in the same year as Amazon.com, and in spite of the fact that they are both Internet companies, eBay is quite different from its supposed competitor. Although similar, the two companies serve different markets and function very differently. Amazon.com chose to signal this difference by the dot com extension, while eBay chose to signal this by the "e" prefix in its name. In fact, the very early version found on an eBay community discussion forum states that the company's initial name was www.Auctionweb.com. [23] A dead link now, the forum discussion page provides some early screen shots of web pages of the initial website.

Second, Amazon.com states its mission to be the "world's most customer-centric company" and "the earth's biggest store." By contrast eBay states its mission is to "provide a global trading platform where practically anyone can trade practically anything." There is a distinct difference between these two missions. Both companies fall under the broad category of virtual marketplaces. However, for Amazon.com clearly the focus is on being a one-stop shop for an online shopping experience; whereas with eBay the company very clearly states that it simply acts as a meeting place where two mutually interested parties can make a trade.

Another unique aspect of eBay is that it encompasses business models within its business models in the form of eBay stores. Businesses and individuals can set up their own eBay frontages and sell items through eBay. While Amazon.com has tried to answer this by creating "zShops," the company has not been as successful as eBay. The reason? Amazon.com represents itself as the shopping place and not the third party businesses that showcase products within it.

While the differences between Amazon.com and eBay are clear, what is the differentiating factor for eBay's success? The enabler, again, is technology. But other differentiators can be debated. We identify its consumers [24] as the primary differentiator with strategy and focus being secondary. This differentiator is also another important difference between Amazon.com and eBay.

For most companies, consumer satisfaction is an objective that is achieved by creating a differentiating business strategy or attribute. However, in the case of eBay, its consumers, or the early adopters who embraced the company website and its methodology in the early years, were also the basis of many important ideas on how the platform should be. While all companies adapt to consumer preferences, for eBay, adaptation has been particularly important because eBay as a company does not have a tangible product to sell. What it sells is an experience. The experience caters to two unique necessities of human beings: the thrill factor and the feel good factor.

The Dec 3, 2001, edition of *Business Week* reveals the secret behind eBay's success. While many attribute it to the business model or technology, the company's founder, Pierre Omidyar, states in an interview: "It was just a matter of communicating to folks what I felt about how people should treat one another, and about how most people feel they should treat one another, just reminding folks of those values and hoping that they would buy into them and live that way."

Essentially, eBay gave consumers the power to design and build the platform in a group setting. We have already discussed how simple the initial web pages of the company were, and most of the communication happened through e-mail. It was through its users that Omidyar got the idea of creating feedback forums that were instantly popular. And when consumer suggestions get implemented on the website, the consumers become loyal to the company and feel a sense of participation in building something meaningful. In addition, the feedback forum brought out the good in individuals. The fundamental principle of human relationships, "Treat others as you want to be treated," started taking hold, and the negative buyers and sellers were automatically filtered out. The challenge of bidding accurately and winning a bid is especially thrilling for those who have never experienced an auction before. Until eBay, this was true for most of the working community. Historically, the word auction has been associated with upper end items that are the privilege of a select few. While auctions of lower end items have existed, they haven't been publicized; hence, an aura of curiosity has always surrounded the word. eBay removed this mystery and allowed one and all to come on one platform to bid.

When you look into it more deeply you realize that the principle behind eBay has been a well-known principle in the business world for a very long time; it's economics 101, the law of supply and demand. Omidyar designed the concept behind a basic principle: to create a level playing field for all, irrespective of their socio-economic or professional status. Economics states that when information is uniformly available to all, the price of a product in an efficient market settles to where the supply equals the demand. Efficient markets are those where information is disseminated evenly and quickly to all. This is exactly what eBay does, and in return, consumers have the power to make a purchasing or selling decision based on the precise information available.

Through all this, technology has been the enabler. With a background in computers and technology, Pierre Omidyar started writing the code for eBay's platform when he was 28 years old. [25] As the company grew, the number of items being sold also grew tremendously. Today you can actually buy anything from inexpensive hats to million dollar personal jets on eBay.

Through this journey of creating history, the company has stayed true to its one focus: a community-based marketplace.

Building a sense of "community" is the key to eBay's success because it is this community feeling that enables millions of individuals to exchange goods based solely on trust. As stated by the founder himself in his interview with *Business Week* senior correspondent Robert D. Hof, "I like to think we're a different kind of big company, because of the way we interact with our community. If we lose that, we've pretty much lost everything."

PERSONAL COMPUTER INDUSTRY:

The Personal Computer, or the "PC" as we now know it, can be singled out as the greatest innovation of the technology era. PC's gave the common man the power to realize his dreams. Visionaries and pioneers of technology often started with a simple idea. Imagine! Had there been no PC, the world would have been deprived of Yahoo, Google, Dell, Amazon.com, eBay and AOL, names that are commonly heard in our homes today.

Do you see the connections here? The improved technology of PC's gave birth to e-companies, and these companies in turn encouraged continuous improvement in PC's. Like any other industry, this industry also carries its unique traits. First and foremost it is an excellent application of the time value of money concept. In layman's terms, this concept refers to assigning a dollar value to the time spent on an activity. Consumers now effectively use computers for a variety of reasons, from researching information, to paying bills, to shopping online.

A second key attribute for the PC industry and for technology in general is the very short (extremely short) product life cycle. Add to this the increased pressure from the consumer to improve attributes, minimize size, improve battery life, and reduce cost to the average consumer, and the PC industry wows us again with all it is able to do. Achieving these objectives is definitely challenging, if not actually monumental.

With every passing year consumers want more value per dollar visible in their PC's. The increased value can be in the form of increased screen size, improved battery life, brighter screens, and additional features, or even a combination of these value items. Further, globalization and free trade across boundaries have allowed manufacturers to tap potential workforce and component suppliers at lower costs. The combined effect has resulted not only in decreasing prices but also with improved features. And the winner is the consumer.

What about the companies? Are they profitable, as well? Yes, company profits are now coming from increased consumer awareness and increased national sales. Moreover, the vast markets within developing nations are really an ocean of consumers willing to spend money on technology. Ironically, Europe, India, and Japan often see the more innovative products first. An example is text messaging. While very popular in the aforementioned countries for the past couple of years, we are only now recognizing the phenomenon in the American market.

The secret of continued increase in market share for the PC manufacturers is quality. Often consumers are willing to pay a premium for quality. Think of Sony vs. Gateway, or Toshiba vs. H-P. However, the consumers who are willing to pay such a premium are often limited to the innovators and early adopters that are typically fifteen-percent of the entire customer base. The first fifteen percent will typically pay a premium for the service as long as the premium is within a tolerable range, and they will be indifferent to any price within that range. The remaining eighty-five percent is comprised of early and late majority, followed by the laggards. These represent the cost-conscious society for whom price plays an important role.

Pricing decisions, especially for new products, are important because they often determine success or failure in most industries. While in the retailing industry pricing played an important role in defining the winning strategies of Wal-Mart vs. Target or Kmart, in the PC industry it defines the success between Microsoft and Apple.

Apple Computers. At this point it is important to make an honest confession: among all the companies studied, Apple presented the most contradictory information. For instance, Apple employees and fans claim they have a superior working platform. So why does Microsoft have ninety-five percent of the market? Our research on Apple Computers began with such questions because the answers constantly defied common logic.

The ancestry of all modern computers goes back to Apple Lisa, a product of Apple Computers, Inc. Apple Lisa 1 was the first computer with a complete graphic interface system and mouse and was priced at $10,000. Steve Jobs, along with his friend Steve Wozniak, designed the first computer that revolutionized the world of PCs. Prior to the PC a computer was an unfriendly machine surrounded by wires and secrecy and often limited to government offices and projects. Apple, under the guidance of its founder Steve Jobs, entered the computer industry at a time when IBM dominated it. At that time the prevalent system was DOS (Disk Operating System), which required a considerable amount of computer literacy to use. DOS was something for specialists.

Though Apple scaled down the computer to make it suitable for a family and to give tremendous computing power to the common man, why is it that the company is often surrounded by negative press? After two decades Apple has captured only a very small percentage of the overall PC market. In an attempt to answer these questions we need to identify the exclusive focus of the company and the factors that have hindered the company's success in the PC market.

The secret behind Apple's distinction probably lies in the underlying philosophy of the company: Apple appeals to the creative masses. As Steve Jobs stated to a group of financial analysts at the recent MacWorld:

> *"We want to stand at the intersection of computers and humanism. Apple was the first computer that…let people who were liberal arts majors use computers and that's part of what is in Apple's DNA …If you really want to understand our company…take some videos of your spouse and your kids, or the guy next door, or whatever, and make an iMovie, and then you will understand. It is the most emotional thing you will have ever done with a computer. You will start to get that we are very intellectual but we appeal to the creative side of things, that humanistic side of things that nobody else in our industry gives a damn about and we do and we love it. We love it so! So that is what's driving us, it's not just making spreadsheets run faster but doing things like iMovie. You gotta [try iMovie] if you really care about understanding this company. It's much more important than crunching your numbers. Trust me on this… I don't have the words to tell you!"* [26]

There are obvious key words in the paragraph above which help to identify the unique differentiator for the company. Additionally, this creative side and humanistic approach to products are also revealed in the company's design philosophy evident in its iMac and G Cube. Look at the vibrant colors! If it was only about colors! Why didn't any other manufacturer imitate the trend? Though opponents laughed and called the approach very feminine, it is true that Apple computers are definitely more interior friendly than the cold designs manufactured by other competitors. While competitors laughed at the use of colors, they realized the importance of design. While staying within the domain of the corporate blue-black color range, competitors did perform re-designs and introduced sleeker, more visually appealing PC's.

It is true that, until recently, Apple often did not introduce new software, but when it decided to do so the end result has been unparalleled. The most recent example can be seen in the tremendously successful iPod, and the most recently announced I-Phone.

Let's continue with the assumption that Apple's distinguishing approach of combining technology with creativity allows the company to create its unique identity. The next question is, why hasn't Apple been able to capture market share from its competitors after being in business for over twenty years? The answer to this question is multi-faceted.

Visibility and incompatibility: these two features go hand-in-hand. Lack of visibility increases incompatibility of other applications to the operating system. Microsoft is present everywhere because in some ways it has chosen to value its distribution channel more than the end user. Once established, the distribution system makes itself an integral part of the market; and by being far more available than Apple's computers, software developers were compelled to design for it. By contrast Apple chose to value the end user experience; however, the company missed the boat on distribution. And being an industry where profits come from the volume sold, distribution plays a decisive role. H-P, for example, chose to establish itself at a discount retailer such as Wal-Mart, partly for the distribution and partly for the supplier volume discounts it can extract.

Aura of secrecy. New products launched by Apple are typically surrounded by an aura of secrecy. This is because unlike Microsoft, which often announces the next upgrade months ahead of launch to encourage wide-scale Beta testing, Apple prefers to do its testing in-house and release only those computers and programs that are known to work. The secrecy approach acts in two ways. First, users have their own expectations; and second, every product introduction becomes a news event. Further, lack of pre-launch information sometimes leads to adverse speculation in the press, which often ends up costing more in value than if the company had chosen to have a structured pre-launch release highlighting the prime features.

As Jobs appropriately stated, Apple caters to the creative side of technology and customers. However, in this process the company misses out on a very important aspect of marketing strategy, and in some ways it is the opposite to what the company set out to do. The first Apple computer brought PC's into the hands of the public, and now if it chooses to cater to a few of the people and not to the masses, that represents a change in strategy. Since the 1990's people have expected to walk into an electronics store and, after spending anywhere from thirty to sixty minutes on research, leave with a computer ready to use at their own convenience. This is not possible with Apple. First, they do not have a wide distribution network, and second, it almost seems that the company has made a conscious effort to separate itself from how the mainstream views it.

Take the example of Apple Stores. The company has 135 retail outlets against Best Buy that opens an average of sixty stores every year. [27] In addition, retail outlets such as Best Buy offer their own service specialists in the form of Geek Squad. These professionals don't deal with any one particular brand; instead, they service everything they sell. This is a tremendous advantage for the manufacturers because they don't have to set up special service and repair relationships locally in every city of presence, but PC companies can access a wide community through retail outlets such as Best Buy. By choosing to go independent with Apple Stores, Apple has eliminated itself from more typical PC availability.

The company started off great, but when the founder of a company chooses to leave, this very act signals internal conflicts and problems. In his absence the company started a downward slide, but with Jobs back at the reins and the introduction of Mac OS and now iPod, Apple seems to be in a position to create the legendary history again. In the last quarter of 2005 the company posted revenue of $5.7 billion, primarily due to the strong sales of its newest venture, the iPod. Apple sold fourteen million iPods in the holiday season alone.

Additionally, the company seems to be finally waking up to its competition by accepting Intel chips in Mac's and designing its ad campaign to highlight this. The ad campaign goes like this:

> *"The Intel chip... for years has been trapped inside PCs, performing dull little tasks when it could have been doing so much more. Starting today, the Intel chip will be set free and get to live life inside a Mac. Imagine the possibilities."* [28]

As the company innovates and introduces new products, market analysts are hopeful that the company is once again set to create history and make a strong comeback to re-capture its position in the world of personal computers.

Dell Computers. As Apple struggled to gain market share from its archrival Microsoft, another entrepreneur was laying the foundation of yet another phenomenon. Michael Dell, in his own domain, (or rather dorm room at the University of Texas in Austin) founded Dell Computers in 1984.

When Dell started his business he was essentially working on upgraded versions of IBM. In 1985 he started selling his own brand, which was built to order. With limited space and cash Dell could not invest in huge inventory, and his solution was to order parts only as and when needed. It was this simple built-to-order system that has expanded to the "Dell Model," a business model that competitors Gateway and Compaq have studied but failed to duplicate.

By 1990 and within only five years of starting operations, Dell was a billion dollar company with access to retail channels through Circuit City, Comp USA, and Price Club outlets. While sales grew, handling and managing the retail channels was not proving to be very cost-effective. In 1994 Dell withdrew his presence from the traditional retail channels and went back to the original focus of the company: direct sales and built-to-order.

This sounds simple and very logical: to order parts when necessary. It removes the need for any warehouse to stock material, no capital is tied up in inventory, and the costs are subsequently lower. Though it sounds simple, the successful execution of such a sophisticated Supply Chain Management model at mass levels requires a high level of technology and competency within the company and within every employee. And it is the successful execution of this model that differentiates it from the competition.

Let's take a quick look at the generic flow of goods for mass produced products vs. built to order parts.

Mass-Produced Products | Built to Order System

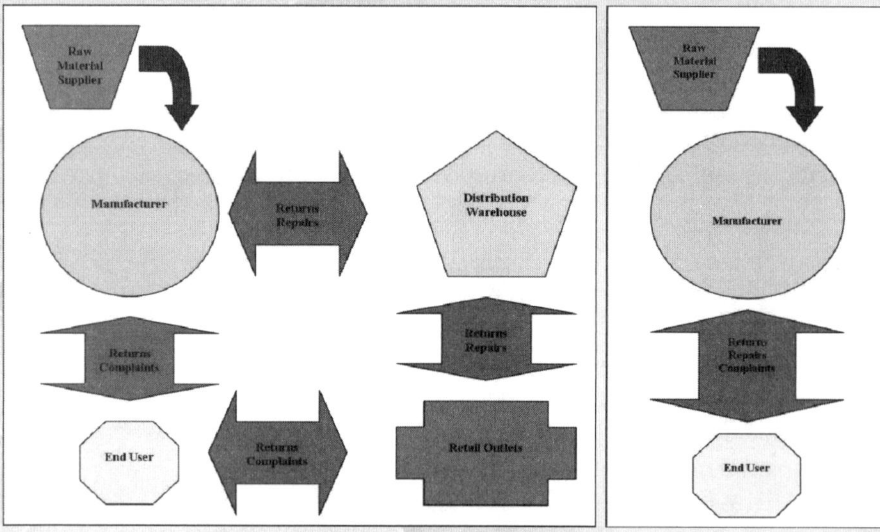

In both instances the retail process ends at the end user, or the consumer; however, what differentiates the two is the means to achieve this. For the mass-produced model, the two links of distribution warehouses and retail outlets translate to inventory and its management at the supplier level. The large inventory is comprised of raw material, work in progress and finished goods; whereas in the built-to-order system the inventory is only work-in-progress.

Since parts are ordered on an as-needed basis, there is no raw material inventory. Finished products are shipped as soon as they are ready. Hence, there is no finished goods inventory. Instead, only work-in-progress is found in inventory. Work in progress inventory for Dell means that it is often traceable to the person who worked on it. At the employee level this translates to greater accountability and responsibility. For the consumer this means consistent quality of products.

Another key aspect of this system compared to mass order is that salesmen communicating directly with their customers often have a much better understanding of customer needs and a better grasp of what trends and innovations are not going to translate to cash cows. In contrast to the $4 billion that its competitor H-P spends on innovation, Dell spends only $440 million. [29] Michael Dell explains that the path of technology products is the same. First, it's the innovators who pay a premium. Then it's the early adopters who still pay a premium (though smaller), and at the other end are laggards who buy when the "mature" product is at the end of its life cycle. Dell is found somewhere in the middle. Once the technology is established Dell steps in with the efficiencies of logistics, and its supply chain adds to its line of products the emerging trends in the market. [30]

If Dell's model is so well understood, why has it not been duplicated? The answer lies in execution, but more importantly the success lies with the founder of the company, Michael Dell. Here's a quick recap of some of the key components of the Dell strategy:

- Keep no inventory. In comparison to its competition, Dell only keeps seven hours of inventory. Precision ordering with a seven-hour window requires a state-of-the-art technology and Supply Chain Management set-up that allows real-time data sharing with suppliers. In addition to this, it also requires very strong and very positive personal relationships with its suppliers.

- Invest in technology to improve with the focus of built-to-order in mind, kind of like what Wal-Mart did for the retailing industry.

- Have an accurate process flow on the shop floor. It sounds similar to the product flow within Wal-Mart distribution centers, where the window from start to finish is twenty minutes.

- Maintain accountability at the employee level since each product can be traced back to who worked on it.

- Provide direct interaction with individual customers through phone and web. Interaction with their corporate customers is the product of a direct sales force and, sometimes, specially designed web pages that cater to one client only.

While all these systems were time-tested principles introduced by the Japanese in the form of JIT inventory management, it was Michael Dell's belief in the system that allowed the company to perfect the model. It took Dell between ten and fifteen years to achieve the level of perfection required to allow the manufacturing process to flow smoothly.

Michael Dell, like Sam Walton and Herb Keller, stayed true to the company focus. He chose NOT to be a jack of all trades but to become the master of one art that he knew well: built-to-order PCs.

Comparatively, it is easier to perceive how technological innovations can and have changed the shopping experience. How can technology possibly influence an industry characterized by heavy fixed assets and costs? The answer is not in the manufacturing industry but rather the airline industry.

CHAPTER 7

AIRLINE INDUSTRY

An airline is an organization that provides transportation services by air route to both passengers and cargo. Passenger carriers can be divided into two types: conventional (or legacy) carriers such as Delta, and low cost carriers (LCC) such as Southwest Airlines. From the first passenger aircraft, The Ford Trimotor in 1925, to the Concorde of the 20th century, the airline industry has been through a variety of technological, business and regulatory changes. Any discussion regarding the airline industry would be incomplete without understanding the unique economics and accounting framework surrounding the industry.

Economics identifies the airline industry as an oligopoly. An oligopoly is a market structure characterized by a only few firms offering a product or service to a broad market. With the number of firms being small, the actions of an individual firm have a sizeable impact on the other firms in the industry. Moreover, an industry comprised of just a few firms also creates the possibility of collusion, creating even greater barriers to entry. For the airline industry, though, collusion should not be confused with a cartel, in which the players collectively decide the course of action. Within the airline industry collusion involves sharing routes, which undoubtedly increases the barriers to entry. A unique trait of airline oligopoly is powerful suppliers and customers. This is unique to airlines because in other oligopolies, such as the automotive industry, the supplier power is not as strong as in the airline industry. This is so because globalization has opened avenues and increased the number of suppliers available. As Airline carriers are few, so are the suppliers. In fact, from a supplier's perspective, it is a monopoly situation. Both the aircraft and the fuel required to fly them are very heavily regulated, and suppliers have the final say. Customers have a variety of suppliers to choose from both within and outside the industry.

Supplementary alternatives to airline travel, like traveling by car, are comparatively inexpensive, especially for short-haul journeys. Furthermore, customers can access competitive pricing through the Internet and have zero switching costs between the different air carriers. Deregulation of the airline industry has translated to relatively low barriers to entry. Despite the heavy up-front investment in equipment and infrastructure, the success of some low cost carriers continues to encourage new entrants in the market, resulting in destructive competition.

During growth periods, equipment-heavy industries tend to over-expand in anticipation of the new demand. The problem is that they all expand. The result is more capacity and fixed (or even lower) demand, resulting in a price war. It's the classical error of circular reasoning. Combine this with the fact that almost all costs for a typical airline are fixed with the only variable component being the cost of carrying one additional passenger. Whether an aircraft built to carry fifty passengers carries twenty passengers or a full load, the cost to the company of flying the aircraft is the same. Figuratively speaking, the difference will not be more than the cost of a can of soda and bag of peanuts for each additional passenger.

Combined effects of the economic factors and world incidents, such as 9/11, have led to increased fuel costs, decreased demand, and very grim profitability for the airline industry. While United Airways, a major legacy carrier, reported a 4Q loss of $182 billion, Delta and Northwest, two of its biggest competitors, continue to face the challenges of bankruptcy restructuring. [31] Low-cost carrier ATA filed for bankruptcy and has not been able to emerge. In fact, ATA recently flew its last flight from its hub city of Indianapolis. Independence Air, another attempt to create a successful low cost carrier, closed doors on January 5th, 2006.

Southwest Airlines. Amid this disappointment, one low cost carrier, Southwest Airlines, continues to grow and make a profit. Why? And even more importantly, how? Historically, the first successful low cost carrier was Pacific Southwest Airlines (PSA), which made its first flight in 1949 and merged with USAir in 1988. The credit for introducing the low-cost carrier model has been given to Southwest Airlines, probably because the company has been able to maintain its profitability and individuality since its birth in 1979.

The Southwest Airlines low-cost carrier model includes:

- A single passenger class.

- A fleet of only two kinds of planes (Airbus A-320's or Boeing 737's) which allows for easy transferability of crew and reduces training and servicing costs.

- A simple fare scheme called Yield Management. The process of Yield Management, also known as revenue management, is the process of understanding, anticipating, and reacting to consumer behavior in order to maximize revenue. Thus, it's quite possible that the passengers who buy their fares ahead of time (often fourteen days) get a better price than those who wait till the last few days. This may seem contrary to common logic; however, often airlines sell seats earlier at a lower price to cover their fixed costs and the seats sold later at a price slightly higher generate more profit. Of course, this strategy works best on popular routes.

- Unreserved seating allows shorter turn-around times because everyone arrives early.

- Providing short flights competes more with car travel.

- Point-to-point routing, avoiding hubs and transfer time.

- Direct sales to customers rather than going through agents, hence saving on agent commissions.

- Multi-tasking employees. This is also the factor that differentiates Southwest Airlines from the crowd.

The Southwest culture is true in every word to the popular proverb: "Time flies when you're having fun." The employees who make this happen are also the company's biggest asset, an asset that adds a lot of intangible good will to the company's balance sheet. They are also an asset that cannot be duplicated easily and one that differentiates the company from its competitors, both legacy carriers and low cost carriers.

Co-founder Herb Keller recognized human resources as an asset and not an expense. Unlike most companies, Southwest Airline's mission statement states, "...Above all, employees will be provided the same concern, respect, and caring attitude within the organization that they are expected to share externally with every Southwest Customer." This is key because most companies within and external to the airline industry talk about customer satisfaction, but very rarely do you see a company making "employee satisfaction" a part of its mission statement. Thus, the management of Southwest also exhibited exceptional foresight when they hedged against fuel, locking in fuel prices at a fraction of the ultimate market cost compared to what its counterparts have paid lately, approximately $26 per gallon, fifty-percent less than the spot market rate. [32]

In addition to acute business planning, the management has also shown exceptional perseverance. The company received considerable resistance from the legacy carriers in its formative years, mainly because of its low-cost pricing. The oligopolistic market structure is heavily governed by signaling. Rather than colluding, many times companies signal to each other the pricing trends to keep uniformity in the industry. Southwest Airlines' pricing challenged this. However, the continued efforts of its management helped to establish the positive company culture by riding out the market turbulence and emerging a winner. Southwest's employees and the other individuals that support the company operations have returned the respect they've received by crediting the airline with the lowest number of customer service complaints per 100,000 customers. The airline industry recognized this high level of customer satisfaction

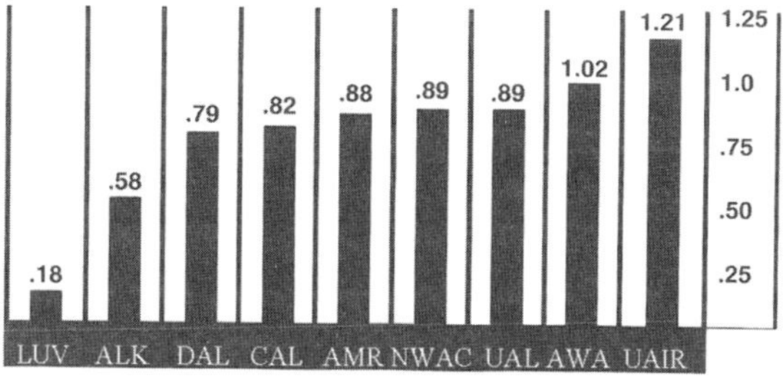

Customer Service Complains per 100,000 customers boarded
for the year ending December 31, 20004

Source: www.southwest.com

through the 2005 Airline Satisfaction Index Study by JD Power and Associates of March 14, 2005. Southwest ranked second in customer service, with Jet Blue taking the lead. [33] *Fortune* magazine, once again, recognized Southwest Airlines as one of America's most admired companies and most admired airlines. [34]

In addition, Southwest also brings out the human element through its exceptional PR. For instance, when Independence Air ceased operations Southwest was the first airline to offer free travel to passengers who held IA's tickets. [35] This move gave it a set of very loyal future customers who will value this company gesture for a long time. Southwest Airlines has taught the uptight and formal airline industry to relax and enjoy a flight, even if it is for business. This, in essence, is the heart of human nature. Parents know that kids learn best when playing, but as adults we try to separate the two upon entering the corporate world. Southwest Airlines has changed this paradigm and continues to stay true to its focus of treating its employees well; in return they have created a working culture that is relaxed and enjoyable. After all, when you enjoy what you do you never have to work.

FedEx. For the airline industry, paradigms did not change in the passenger sector alone. They have changed tremendously in the cargo sector as well, as seen in FedEx Group of Companies (FedEx). As in the passenger sector, the cargo sector also has a few major players with some other smaller players mixed in. There are two, however, which take the majority of the market: FedEx and UPS. While competing for business with other carriers, these companies also compete for business with the postal services of respective countries, including the US Postal Service. Because there are two major players that decide how this game is played, this is an effective monopoly situation. It could also be argued that it is technically an oligopoly industry with prominent traits of monopoly markets. Monopoly markets are typically utility or energy sectors in which the barriers to entry are very high and the companies, themselves, are highly-regulated. While the barriers to entry are high for the cargo airline, global deregulation of air space has allowed the industry to expand its horizons.

FedEx was a Yale University research project by its founder, Fred Smith. In those times the idea of overnight delivery of packages seemed not only far-fetched but also so nearly impossible that Smith's project was awarded a grade of C. [36] Despite the low enthusiasm shown by his professor, Fred Smith did not forget his paper, even during the intensity of the Vietnam War (in which he served after graduating). He studied the logistics of the military and how the packages were delivered to the soldiers, fully realizing the importance of on-time and speedy delivery in such dire conditions. He returned to the US hoping to convert his research into a successful business. In 1971 he started his express transport business in Little Rock, Arkansas. Two years later the company had its first night of continuous operations when 386 employees and a fleet of fourteen jets delivered 186 packages overnight to twenty-five cities, rightfully earning Fred Smith the title "Father of the Overnight Delivery Business."

While this sounds impressive, the company lost $27 million in its first two years of operations. Nevertheless, the company that was close to bankruptcy in the initial years of operation reported an increase of thirty-three percent in its net income for 2005 ($471 million) compared to $354 million in 2004. [37] Unlike many success stories, Fred Smith did not create this company by chance. It was a well-planned research paper that he put into practice. For starters he realized that borrowing cargo space in passenger airlines would not satisfy the on-time necessity of overnight deliveries. So he decided to have his own fleet. One of his key innovations was to apply the hub and spoke distribution pattern to reduce costs. This also allowed him to cover more locations than his competitors. [38]

The hub for FedEx was the Memphis International Airport, and the spokes were routes directly emerging and ending at this hub. This pattern was so effective that competition was forced to follow. Delta pioneered this for the passenger sector by choosing Atlanta, Georgia, as its hub. Being a visionary and an avid reader of history, Fred Smith was able to look at the cargo industry from a different perspective. He realized that the delivery of packages, while technically cargo, is essentially the task of providing companies and individuals with vital tools to complete their tasks.

These tools could be in the form of a business letter or crucial medical equipment needed across national and international borders. By identifying the company as a vital link between borders, Smith correctly captured the success determinants for the company. He also realized it was very important for his team to know the exact whereabouts of every package, along with expected time of delivery, at any time. In order to do this he made technology his partner. While the credit for the company's success definitely goes to its founder, the factor that differentiated FedEx from the crowd was its capability to integrate across its value net, not only at the competition level but also at the consumer level. **The value net for FedEx, or for that matter any company in this industry, is unique for the following reasons:**

- Its consumers are also its clients.
- While suppliers have a high bargaining power, the relationship between the company (FedEx) and its suppliers is symbiotic and reduces the restrictions often imposed by high bargaining power.
- Any kind of alliance with complementary industries will only be beneficial for the complementors; therefore, resistance to merging or creating other synergies is minimal.
- The supplementary industries or competitors do not gain from the "price wars." Fixed costs in the form of delivery trucks, technology centers and hubs are once again high, and price wars will cut into the profits of everyone.

With this background, the FedEx acquisition of Caliber Systems, Inc., is easier to comprehend. Caliber provided JIT delivery and transportation management solutions. From a value net perspective, Caliber is a complementary company. By its acquisition FedEx consolidated its position along the horizontal frame, leaving little room for rivals to compete. Another important acquisition for FedEx has been Kinko's. Kinko's, a privately held firm, changed how the corporate world presented and organized information.

In 2003 FedEx purchased Kinko's in a $2.4 billion cash deal. By acquiring Kinko's, FedEx achieved two objectives. First, it once again consolidated its position across the value net and left little room for the existing customers of Kinko's to ship from another carrier. Second, and probably more important for the 21st century, it extended its ground delivery system to the e-world. Aptly put by FedEx spokesman, Jess Bunn: "For years FedEx was in the physical delivery of documents, but now we are moving into the electronic delivery of documents. Kinko's receives electronic documents and prints them out. The logical extension is to have them delivered by FedEx." [39]

While creating harmony with its partners, FedEx did not forget its supplementer's competitors. In July 2004 FedEx created an alliance with USPS to ship Global Express Guaranteed, the USPS version for on-time international delivery. This alliance with FedEx replaced a previous contract with DHL. [40] The shipping labels carried both the USPS and FedEx logos; and, keeping the business model of USPS in mind, there were no shipping increases due to its alliance. By thinking intuitively, FedEx reduced competition constructively. Integration with complementary companies is intuitive; what is not intuitive is integration at the consumer level.

Source: www.cbsmarketwatch.com

FedEx, however, did not forget its customer. Recognizing the ease of use at customer level, the company gave proprietary software to relevant customers. The software allowed them to print shipping labels. FedEx would receive the pick up information electronically, ship, and then deliver the parcel. The authors of "FDX Group: Building the Electronic Commerce Backbone for the Future" write about the unique example of its "merge in transit" service, which was customized to customers that needed it. Micron Computers had such a service. Under this program FedEx actually stored accessories such as printers in its hub; and, upon receiving the shipping information electronically from Micron, FedEx employees would match the accessory to the computer and deliver it to the end user. It is such differentiating changes along its value net that led FedEx to change the shipping norms in the corporate and consumer world.

While the vision and continued involvement of its founder has played a vital role in the company's success, it is important to remember its most valued asset: its employees. Fred Smith created an environment of empowering his employees by giving them an opportunity to participate and make suggestions. The result was increased loyalty, which allowed FedEx to capture market share from UPS during UPS' union troubles. The UPS strike resulted in 800,000 extra packages per day for FedEx. Thousands of FedEx employees continued to work beyond their scheduled times to meet the challenge. As a result, after the UPS strike FedEx had captured an amazing forty-three percent of the total market. The company continues to expand its horizons by having recently entered the China market. [41] And with solid stock performance, the company continues to establish new avenues to retain its leadership in the delivery services industry. Being true to his passion for history "... FedEx CEO Frederick Smith, who says he has learned far more from historical figures than from trendy leadership gurus," [42] has created history himself.

In an industry that is dominated by so called "geeks" or technology-savvy professionals, innovation seems intuitive. What happens to innovation in an industry that is dominated by endless amounts of paperwork and where academic theories play a very important role?

CHAPTER 7

HEALTH CARE INDUSTRY:

Medicine, or the field of medical sciences, encompasses a multitude of professionals and businesses: insurance companies, pharmacies, doctors and their staffs, medical equipment producers, drug manufacturers, and let's not forget the most important link: the patient. Unlike other service sectors and the manufacturing industry, unfortunately, the field of medicine has very rarely listened to its customer: the patient. It is actually ironic, considering the fact that medicine is mostly about preventing, minimizing, or repairing physical and mental human tragedies. One would think that placing customer service at the center of health care would be the most important aspect of medical practice for both doctors and hospitals. While it is true that medical advances have increased life expectancy and that mortality rates are low, it is also true that the labyrinth of rules surrounding the industry has left the patient totally confused and helpless.

Insurance companies only spell out the good stuff in bold, and often the most important part is printed so small that it seems completely unimportant. Instead of the doctors deciding the treatment, unbiased by any aspect, it is often the insurance implications that decide the course of treatment for most patients. Whether the patient takes the generic or the name brand of a medication is governed by the pharmacy coverage he has. And companies in general encourage their employees to consider generic brands, which are just as good but less expensive. So, with an industry where total chaos once ruled it was only a matter of time before technology would step in and again demand more control.

WebMD. This demand came in the form of a company called WebMD, a name that says it all. Its roots go back to the California-based company, Healtheon. [43] Founded by Netscape founder Jim Clark, Healtheon merged with WebMD in 1999 to form Healtheon WebMD. It's interesting to note that founders of both companies,

Jim Clark and Jeffery Arnold, are no longer associated with the merged company.

When Jim Clark developed the idea of Healtheon his single objective was to "fix the US health care system." [44] This vision, coupled with the forming of WebMD, captured the attention of major technology players and the health care industry. Examples include the Microsoft partnership in 1999 for $250 million, and its agreement with Google in which the company provides sponsored search links relevant to the health care industry.

It would be wrong to say that WebMD was the first attempt to integrate technology and the Internet in the field of medicine. A prior effort called Physicians Online Network (POL) provided valuable information and access to doctors only, once again leaving out the patient. WebMD chose to change this. It was the first website that actually took all the information typically presented in medical jargon and translated it into language that the consumer can understand. This is also the unique aspect that differentiates the company from its competition.

Unlike its predecessors POL, DrKoop.com, and drug company Pfizer's attempts to compete head on with WebMD [45], attempts that specifically targeted either physicians or insurance companies, WebMD chose to empower the consumer. Knowledge has an immensely powerful ripple effect. While ignorance is considered bliss in many situations, ignorance in matters of healthcare can mean death. WebMD changed this. By providing free access to a large pool of knowledge and resources the company eliminated any excuse a patient could find for not educating himself/herself about individual health issues. The website provided a platform for doctors, patients, and insurance companies to create synergies. It allowed patients to research medical subjects easily and authoritatively, making them more aware of the issues concerning their health. This also enabled them to ask more direct and pointed questions, translating to better health decisions. The website provided patients with an avenue to find alternatives and resources available for more difficult medical conditions, such as kids with Downs Syndrome or adults facing the threat of cancer.

For doctors WebMD presented an avenue to continue education, research medical databases and forums to discuss recent developments in their fields of specialty, and to evaluate their applications and success rates within the industry. The company's most recent acquisition of eMedicine.com, Inc., further reinforces this attribute. On Jan 18, 2006, WebMD acquired eMedicine.com for the purchase price of $25.5 million and, in turn, provided its customer base with access to in-depth coverage for over 6000 topics. The coverage not only provides theoretical background, it also provides doctors and health care professionals with clinical information related to diagnosis and treatment. [46]

Since its inception the website has emerged into more of a community feeling rather than being a dry "info-mediary." The company platform is a vertical portal with two subsets, a public and a private. The public portal essentially provides free access to a wealth of information available to anyone who accesses the website. For the private portal WebMD provides an integrated platform for both employers and health plan management companies, which allows members to understand their benefits and coverages specific to their needs so they can make more informed decisions.

Whereas transferring the knowledge base to consumers was a vital distinguishing feature, the company's continued success is attributed to the string of acquisitions and mergers. The acquisitions effectively allowed the company to survive the dot.com bust and emerge a winner. In 2001 the company purchased a major competitor, Medscape, and also acquired companies such as Envoy that were active in the business of processing electronic claims. With the purchase of Medical Manager, the company developed a new line of business practice management software for physicians' offices. The company received immense credibility when California Public Employees' Retirement System (CalPERS) backed its $100 million debt. With this backing and its strong initial cash position, the company continues with its acquisitions, the most recent one being eMedicine.com, Inc.

From a revenue model perspective, WebMD essentially has three avenues: the clearinghouse through WebMD Envoy, sales of its practice management software, and its network services. The company also has a publishing division. As stated on the company website, the list of publications includes *The Little Blue Book*, a physician directory, *ACP Medicine and ACS Surgery: Principles of Practice*, medical reference textbooks, and *WebMD the Magazine.* The magazine is a free publication distributed to physicians' offices.

From a model perspective, the public portal provides free access; however, the private portal is fee- or subscription-based. In essence, what we have seen is the evolution of the customer-centric attitude in the medical industry as well. Thanks to initiatives such as WebMD, the consumer (patient) is more educated and more confident in asking questions. But the innovation in the world of medicine does not stop at WebMD; it goes beyond that. The beginning of 2006 has seen a lot of attention being focused on the American health care system.

The Economist's January 28th edition released a special report titled "Desperate Measures." In addition to emphasizing the legacy of the Second World War behind the current healthcare system, *The Economist* report states that American spending on health care has always been ahead of income growth. Businesses are reducing benefits or increasing deductibles and co-pays as medical costs increase. Their rationale is that if the consumer or patient pays more out-of-pocket expenses, the services will be used more cautiously. While this is true, it is also hinting at the changing attitude towards the industry. This change is moving the industry more towards commercialization. Health care providers and reformers need to remember that the closer it gets to commercialization, the sooner the influences of commercialization will begin to infiltrate the system. As indicated earlier, forty-seven million Americans are uninsured, with premium increases of eighty-one percent since 2000. As a comparison, we spent $5,267 per capita on healthcare, $1,821 more than Switzerland, the nearest runner-up.

For instance, if medical procedures get too expensive then patients may choose to have non-emergency procedures outside the USA. Medical transcription is very commonly outsourced to developing economies, such as India. Whereas healthcare providers are cutting back on benefits, certain legislative efforts by states attempt to limit this. Maryland, for instance, has a new law that requires all large employers to spend at least eight percent of their payrolls on health care. These additional costs could change the economic scenario for many companies. Businesses that can do so may choose to cease operations or limit the number of employees in certain high cost locations.

Though surrounded by an array of great challenges that health care reform generates, the innovation in the industry has not stopped. A recent illustration of the increased consciousness on health issues is the company www.myfoodphone.com. The company is a pioneering effort by its parent company, NATS Inc., a mobile-health application service provider. MyFoodPhone's website claims it is "the world's first camera-phone/food-journaling feedback loop that links individuals with their own nutrition coaches and advisors." [47] Another illustration is Zotec Solutions, Inc., [48] based in Carmel, Indiana. The company makes software that allows consumers to pay health care bills and to update their insurance details online. Founded in 1998, the company introduced its "EZ Med Portal," a secured pay platform that consumers can access from a physician's office website or through information provided in the paper bill.

Zotec, MyFoodPhone, and WebMD are all examples of the continued effort to organize the health care industry. And more importantly, it is a trend that hints towards the commercialization of the industry and of health care services. Just as history repeats itself, business logic also repeats itself across industries.

The logic of lean manufacturing and low cost airlines is catching up with the health care system, also. The article "India: World's Preferred Healthcare Destination" describes the outsourcing of medical operations. Already the practice of outsourcing radiology and medical transcription is very popular for two reasons: cost savings and time difference. The time difference between the two countries allows doctors to get analyses in less than twenty-four hours. When the US sleeps, India wakes up; so while the patients and doctors here in the US are resting, their counterparts in India are working on the transferred assignments. If health care costs in the western world keep soaring, it is only a matter of time before patients will look for alternate answers.

These changing trends are opening new paths to explore for all entities involved, be it the payer, the provider, or the insurer. In times to come it will be interesting to see the direction the industry takes. While technology makes much of what was once impossible possible, the one aspect that is very difficult to digitize is the "feel aspect." Thus, industries predominantly categorized by the human side have faced bigger challenges, as can be studied through the history of Amazon, eBay or WebMD.

Another industry where putting a face to the name has been vital is the field or science of recruitment. A division of HR, recruitment has often been considered to be one of the most mundane and time consuming of business activities. Monster.com chose to change this attitude and make recruitment, or e-recruitment, just as exciting and enticing as shopping online.

EMPLOYMENT ADS:

The traditional practice of recruitment involved advertising, screening resumes received either through fax or snail mail, and then the interview process. The time frame for starting interviews typically remains anywhere from thirty to forty-five days, depending on the cutoff date for sending in resumes. This process is standardized until the actual task of selection enters the scene. While simple, the task also involves a considerable number of man-hours in sorting through resumes and paperwork. Just as technology was revolutionizing consumer experiences in shopping and traveling, it was set to redefine the process of online recruitment. This industry competes against different recruitment consultants as well as traditional in-house hiring.

Monster. Founded in 1967, Monster Worldwide Inc. (formerly called TMP Worldwide Inc.) is the parent company of Monster.com, the online recruitment leader. Monster.com, formed in 1994 as the Monster Board, emerged at the same time as Amazon.com and eBay.com. The timing for the company launch was perfect. The company began as a simple jobs board for posting resumes and searching job listings. It has now evolved into a leading provider of comprehensive recruitment solutions to recruitment consultants, employers, and job seekers alike.

The candidates typically do not pay for posting resumes. The fee structure is for employers and consultants trying to find the right match for a job posting. The fee allows one to post a job and also search the database. The company also provides a feature to network with people. Monster.com's initial portal was very simply designed to bring job seekers and providers together in a common virtual location. Though simple, the idea was new. The company's continued success can be attributed to the novelty of the concept as well as to its strong parental history and established track record in the field of recruiting services. As the company progressed it evolved into an HR portal.

However, the model was easily replicable. This is probably an example of a company where the first move advantage or the novelty of the idea did not carry the company too far. Competition caught up. Recognizing the growing trend of online recruitment, many players jumped in - including established players such as Yahoo Jobs. With the wide array of competition from newspaper websites to professional organizations to independent company and recruiter websites, the choices available to the job seeker were plentiful. Furthermore, Monster.com started off as a very simple and generic portal. The newer companies were more focused, and some specialized in temporary jobs while others catered to specific qualifications and salary ranges. Though well-organized, the procedure for uploading a resume was cumbersome and time consuming. The later versions of online recruitment websites were able to cut down on this by allowing other options, such as e-mailing resumes directly to recruiters and employers.

Monster.com became associated with very generic positions that did not add much value to the company, and while it was a good resource it did not provide much value to the job seeker in the long run. This is now changing. The company's effort to promote the website into a portal with networking options, discussion boards, and the latest relevant research to job seekers remains strong. To employers it offers an array of solutions ranging from being their partner for campus recruitment to legal compliance to employee diversity strategies. These changes clearly indicate the company's intention to become a one-stop shop portal for all recruitment solutions for both employers and job seekers. As geographical barriers diminish and stereotypes about developing countries vanish, resources such as Monster.com will prove invaluable for companies because they will have the entire world as a possible talent pool to search. In turn it will give immense opportunities to job seekers to expand their professional and cultural horizons by working in different countries.

SUMMARY:

There are multiple morals to the stories presented here. Though each story may differ on the surface, a deeper consideration shows that the New Economy is an evolution of the Old Economy. Therefore it would be wise for businesses not to discard those principles completely. For starters, the first obvious moral is that change is constant. The players in the Old Economy knew this; but in the past, change came more in the form of political or economic variations. Within the New Economy the entire concept or thought process is challenged, and a new way of thinking promotes experimentation, sometimes with success and sometimes with failure. Failure, however, does not deter continued innovation. This is the hallmark of the New Economy.

Greater avenues of expression have allowed the smallest inventors to put their ideas forward. Take the example of stay-at-home moms, intelligent women who decide to take a break from traditional employment in order to devote time to their families. Recognizing the need for balance, many women have decided to start home businesses in fields as varied as designing greeting cards to providing financial solutions for individuals and smaller businesses. Home-based business, and even the very idea of working from home, was scoffed at not too long ago, and now businesses are allowing employees to work from home in order to accommodate different lifestyles and expectations from employers and employees alike.

Secondly, though in different industries, the companies have and need to maintain a symbiotic relationship. They are all linked to e-commerce in one form or another through the Internet, and if one business gets a "thumbs up" the competing businesses get recognition as well. And fortunately the reverse situation can be beneficial for competition. For instance, in recent months, as investors have raised questions about Google, the focus has shifted back to Yahoo and to comparisons with Google.

The third moral here is that with every single day the world is getting smaller, literally. Consumers have endless choices with no switching costs; they are more educated, they know exactly what they want, and they are not afraid to voice their requests. And if businesses do not respond quickly, web- savvy consumers are willing to take the additional step to jump ship.

The best example here is found in the health care industry. Patients who cannot afford the expense of Western medicine are researching alternatives in other parts of the world through the Internet and then traveling to foreign lands and receiving equal, if not better, treatment. While all the talk and the research and the shift from a manufacturing-based economy to a knowledge- or creative-based economy is true, it is also true that at the end of the day businesses exist to make a profit. Businesses are constantly seeking to increase market share and reach out to new consumers. The New Economy approaches to achieving these goals are constantly being refined and redefined, but the human element predominant in many of the Old Economy companies, such as GM and Ford, is coming back in a new way. Earlier companies created returns to society by taking extra care of their employees; today companies are creating similar returns to society in much grander philanthropic ways, and investors, the public, are now demanding ways of recognizing this. Consequently, though the gap between the Old Economy and the New Economy seems wide, the transition is simply a process of natural evolution.

CHAPTER 8

The New Economy: A New Way of Thinking

"Ill blows the wind that profits nobody."

– William Shakespeare,
Henry VI

CHAPTER 8

There is a common expression about being on the "wrong side of the equation." To find yourself on the wrong side of the equation means that you are in a passive position with no power or influence or leverage; whereas being on the right side of the equation equals a position of power, leverage and influence.

Definition: equation /I'kweizn/noun

A statement showing that two amounts or values are equal, for example 2X+y=54. This result can be changed with other mathematical expressions added to the equation depending on ***the side of the equation to which they are added!***

However, an equation can also be described as something that is favorable due to leverage. The form of the leverage can vary widely, such as:

- A unique set of contacts
- Time or speed with which something can be accomplished
- Unique or difficult to obtain knowledge
- Technology which enables improvement in productivity or efficiency

- Standard Templates to enable others to take advantage of existing or past knowledge

Other examples of leverage might include the following:

- Invention Patents. The invention process takes place only once, but the ongoing production of the idea can literally be forever.

- Musical Artist DVD's, CD's Tapes, or Seminars, where something is created just once and where it is possible to leverage this and distribute this to many others at no additional effort or expense.

- Movies which may appear unprofitable at first can become profitable later if the cost of making it one time are exceeded by the revenue from showing it many times.

These are simple examples of the fundamental changes taking place in the work place, changes which have the potential to provide great leverage in income in comparison to the effort required. The above positions are examples of working on the right side of the equation.

Examples of those occupations on the wrong side of the equation would include occupations such as carpenter, plumber, electrician, sales clerk, or salaried (non-commissioned) salesmen, where the input and output are directly proportional and offer no leverage opportunity.

Everyone dreams about retiring or having a lot of money to do whatever he or she wants. This book describes how changes in government policies, new legislation, and technology, business, and government strategy have created impact on employees in many different industries and geographies. Layoffs, outsourcing, downsizing, and loss of pensions are just a few of the events discussed here. Such events have made employees vulnerable, disenfranchised, and unmotivated; and continuing to work as an employee in fact, in some cases, could be worse. A salaried or hourly employed worker has no leverage and can be described as being on the wrong side of the equation.

Currently this country is still adjusting to change and to New Economy concepts, whether this manifests itself in the price of oil, the cost of war in the Middle East, the loss of pensions, or the increase in medical bills. Therefore, this book is particularly timely as a way for Americans to consider alternative options to escape being an employee. By becoming innovators and entrepreneurs, Americans are fighting back by doing what they are best known for. For the unemployed, or those employed but in dead-end jobs, this book provides the answers regarding what to do and how to improve their lives!

Many people have continued to work in traditional occupations for conventional companies in the mistaken belief that a regular salary, health care benefits, and a pension represented security. But this kind of "security" has proven to be something of a mirage. Many of these individuals have missed the largest technological shifts and changes in our time and are, therefore, on the wrong side of the equation.

The remaining chapters explore the differences between being on the right and wrong sides of the equation, and we examine this phenomenon with real world examples of companies and individuals who are operating successfully on the right side of the equation. Today it seems to be harder than ever to make a living and to make ends meet without going deeper into debt. Being on the wrong side of the equation is becoming tougher and tougher to avoid.

CHAPTER 8

We will show employees why it no longer makes financial sense to work as a W2 employee but rather to become self-employed in a situation that offers leverage and the opportunity to be on the right side of the equation. Be prepared to consider your future, and dare to make changes with the help of hard, pragmatic advice on how you can survive in the New Economy.

CHAPTER 9

The Future As We See It

"You should have feared false times when you did feast."

– William Shakespeare,
Timon of Athens

CHAPTER 9

Albert Einstein once said, "I never think of the future. It comes soon enough." Likewise, Abraham Lincoln once said, "The best thing about the future is that it only comes one day at a time." Einstein, a scientist, and Lincoln, the sixteenth president of the United States, were both visionaries in two seemingly dissimilar professions in two vastly different ages, yet their ideas about the future are similarly different. For one the future comes too soon, and the other reminds us our future arrives day by day, giving us ample opportunity to learn from the past and improve upon the present to secure a better future for both ourselves and the generations to come.

Much has been prophesied about the future of individual countries and the world in general. However, most of this discussion has centered on economics. Which nation will dominate the world economy in 2010? Will the US continue to be a superpower? Or will the third-world countries of the past be the first-world countries of the New Economy? These are some of the questions many are asking, and academicians, economists, business leaders, and politicians alike are finding ways to answer them.

Unfortunately, the discussions have centered on the broad category of commerce and finance. What about global warming and the change in weather patterns? Recent elections in the US promised to redefine the education system and provide both young and adult students the skills to compete in the new global economy. Are we achieving this? What about the next generation of schoolchildren and the "baby boomer" generation? Are their skills equal to the opportunities of today and tomorrow? Can we re-engineer the future workforce in time?

In this book some vital and pertinent social issues are highlighted Because the New Economy is about people. It is not about increasing barriers but about decreasing barriers to better economic performance. Essentially the world, which was earlier divided by man, is now once again merging to meet the challenges. We first fought wars to separate ourselves and gain land. We successfully drove the natives of this land into reserved areas, and today we are again fighting wars to free other nations so their people can lead a life that we think is better. At the same time we talk about creating synergies and partnerships across the globe. **More specifically we look at the following issues:**

- US as a Credit Society
- Decline of Manufacturing
- Increasing Dependence on Petroleum Products
- Natural Disasters – Mother Nature Taking Control?
- The US Society – Ignorant or Arrogant?
- Economy: Entity or Concept?

The above topics will be discussed with emphasis on the US economy, but we will also see how the seemingly different social issues, weather pattern changes, individual actions and the culture and attitude of a country as a whole can influence its economy in much greater ways than government reform.

US AS A CREDIT SOCIETY:

We start off with Economics 101. The popular notion is that either the government or the Federal Reserve controls the economy. This is true to an extent, but let's take a deeper look into this subject. What does the Federal Reserve control and how? "The Fed is likely to cut interest rates again," was a sentence heard one too many times in the booming economy. Well, if "the Fed" cuts the interest rate, for individuals the incentive to save decreases and for businesses the incentive to borrow increases. It is this balance of saving and borrowing that "the Fed" tries to control, and in the process it makes sure the seesaw of saving and borrowing remains in a state of approximate equilibrium. Savings come from households and individuals. Though indirect, essentially it is households and business firms that control the economy, not the government. The government is also a kind of business entity with its own trade balances, debts, and surpluses, an entity that enforces rules and regulations to ensure fair trade. Households control the inputs required by firms to build or provide goods and services, and in return for these resources firms provide the households (individuals) with income, which is in turn used to buy the finished products these firms produce. While there is no sure way for us to know what the Fed really thinks about the outlook for the current year and beyond, based on logical reasoning it would be accurate to state that the three possible areas for the Fed to be concerned are employment and output growth, inflation and interest rates, and the role of the government in influencing them.

One of the key indices keenly observed by the Fed is the PCE, or Personal Consumption Expenditures. You probably thought of the Consumers' Price Index (CPI), but that's "old school." Remember we are talking about the New Economy. And just as the New Economy changed the rules of doing business, it also changed the rules of measuring inflation. [49] The PCE is a measure of price changes in

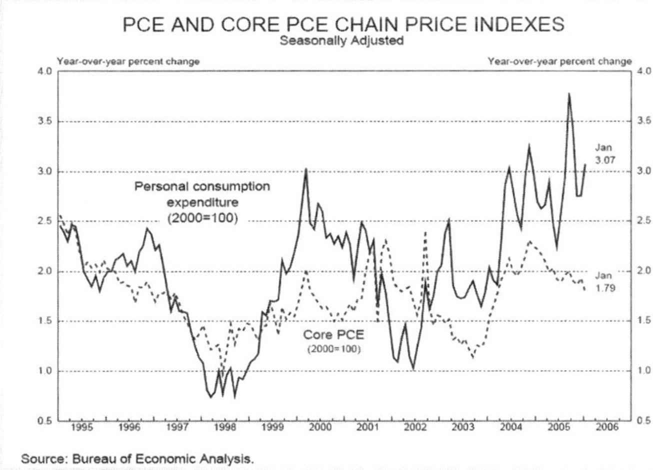

consumer goods and services used or consumed by individuals. While this is similar to CPI, the main difference is that the CPI uses a fixed basket of goods whereas the PCE reflects the change in buying patterns of consumers.

For example, when a hurricane destroys oranges in Florida, resulting in a price increase, people buy more apples. The PCE reflects this change in buying pattern. It is also the largest component of the GDP (Gross Domestic Product). The GDP, as we know, is the summation of consumption, government spending, net exports, and investments. PCE is consumption. Every month, the Bureau of Economic Analysis releases the data

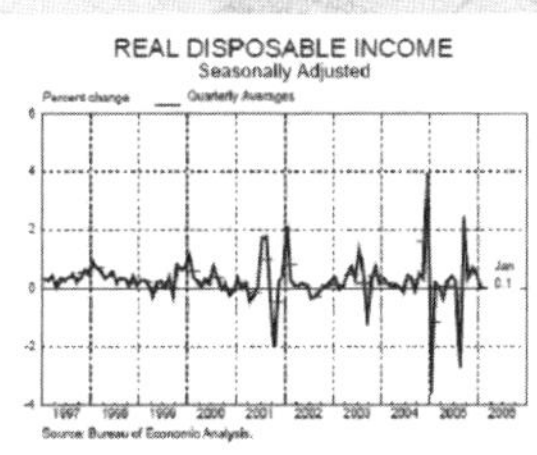

entitled Personal Income and Outlays. The data trails the prior two months and, in the corresponding graph, represents the January 2006 numbers. Analyze the above data in relation to the personal savings rate and real disposable income below. Notice how the two figures are headed towards the red. It is important to understand the fine line of difference here.

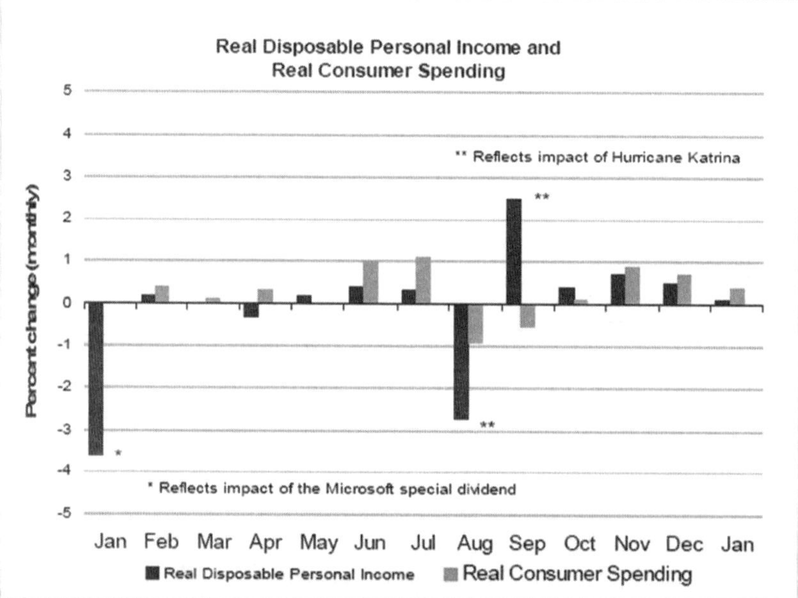

Broadly, real disposable income is the "wages" less the "taxes;" whereas "savings" is income available after deducting the necessary consumption from disposable income. In other words, low disposable income is a result of either low wages and/or increased taxes, and a decline in savings is either because prices have increased or needs have increased. The PCE chart indicates that the core PCE was at 1.79%. It is at the upper end of the acceptable range of one to two percent, but it is still within a comfortable range.

The calculation of core inflation excludes energy and food prices as they are fluctuating. While (economically speaking) the rationale of consumers switching between more expensive and less expensive foods may be true, the reality is that when the price of milk increases consumers do not replace it with lemonade. The cuts come, but not in the grocery list; they come in other luxury items such as going to the movies or dining out. The core inflation that is popularly used and reported excludes food and energy prices, whereas it includes other shopping patterns which see reduced spending in inflationary times.

To continue the discussion, let's go ahead with the assumption that PCE is a true measure of consumer spending and changing habits. As can be seen through the next chart, we are obviously spending more than we are earning. So, where is the money coming from? Credit, of course! The low interest rates, combined with the real estate boom, have been a blessing to our spending society.

Look at the opposite trends here and all logic and rationale fails to explain it. On one hand we complain of a tight labor market, wage pressures, and individuals losing jobs. And on the other hand the country sees continued increases in consumer spending.. As a nation we are so used to the concept of credit that buying by actually writing a check seems too old fashioned now. How many of us actually write a check today? Very few. Why? It is just so inconvenient. While many use debit cards, the increased marketing by credit card companies to offer mileage, reward points and the like for every dollar spent with a card has increased the use of credit cards, resulting in increased levels of debt.

Take a look at the next chart. Notice the upward trend. This is how a yield curve of a successful economy should look, not the debt burden. Notice that the chart separates the mortgages and consumer credit debt. The steep increase in mortgage is another sign that we are refusing to see.

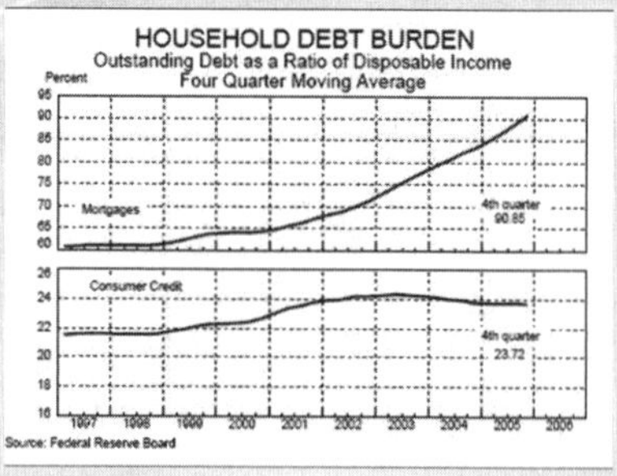

Low interest rates have allowed individuals to buy houses beyond their means. Additionally, lenders and builders alike advertise houses based on mortgage payment per month. The logic says, why waste a thousand dollars in rent when you can own a house for only a marginal increase, and in some states no increase, and take advantage of interest tax deduction as well? In all the excitement of being homeowners, many forget to add the taxes, the community dues, the increased energy bills, and the additional cost of maintaining a house versus apartment living. The result is that people begin living beyond their means. *When individuals and the society start living beyond their means, it is no surprise that the government of the United States is living beyond its means, too*

Many people fail to recognize that the government as a whole is also a business entity with its own targets. The different divisions of a government can be considered as different business units. For a successful business conglomerate, while the sales and profit targets can vary from one business unit to another it is important that the core business value run across all units, and very often that is the case. Unfortunately governments don't work with the same efficiency or philosophy. Very often the sharing of information and resources is restricted due to bureaucracy.

As the world economies try to merge, the need to share is growing both inter- and intra-governmentally. The world's mission to rid itself of terrorism requires immense levels of information sharing. For starters, if the multitudes of federal agencies agree to share intellectual information among themselves they could save time, effort, and money that is often wasted in duplication of projects. Increased spending by the U.S. government has created the largest budget deficit in recent memory. Take a look at the numbers:

- The US current account deficit increased to $804.9 billion in 2005 from $668.1billion in 2004.
- Current account is the combined net surplus or deficit of goods and services, income and net unilateral current transfers.
- The deficit on goods and services increased to $723.6 billion in 2005 from $617.6 billion in 2004.
- The deficit on goods is $781.6 billion compared to $ 665.4 billion in 2004.
- The surplus on services increased to $58.0 billion in 2005 from $47.8 billion in 2004.
- Income surplus decreased to $1.6 billion in 2005 from $30.4 billion in 2004.
- Unilateral current transfers (as net outflows) were $82.9 billion compared to $80.9 billion in 2004.
- As a share of the US GDP, the current deficit increased to 6.4 percent in 2005 compared to 5.7 percent in 2004.[50]

On reading the details of the current account deficit through the Bureau of Economic Analysis website at **www.bea.gov** some interesting points emerge. For starters it is interesting to note that the increased deficit in goods and services accounted for most of the total current account deficit. Within goods and services it is no surprise that imports of goods far exceeded exports, and within that classification the largest contribution was by China. US imports from China totaled $243 billion, making it the second largest partnership after Canada at $288 billion. [51] At the going rate, the difference of a mere $45 billion will disappear probably within a short span of two to three years. Every coin has two sides. While the US carries a trade deficit, China's trade surplus with the United States increased by 24.5% in 2005 to $202 billion. [52]

It is also important to note that, within goods and services, while goods were running a deficit services ran a surplus of $58 billion. However, understanding the possible positive implications of this trend is key to the success of the United States in the new emerging economy. Briefly speaking it is fair to assume that it will take a considerable amount of re-investment and effort for the manufacturing industry in the US to regain its glory days. However, the country can still continue to maintain its edge and supremacy in the business world by investing in what some call creative economy and some call knowledge economy. This is essentially investing in intellectual capital and strengthening one's hold in the service sector, be it consulting, finance or research and development.

This brings us to the third component, income. While income shows a surplus of $1.6 billion in 2005, note the difference. In 2004 this surplus was $30.4 billion. What this means is that those payments being made on foreign-owned assets have increased substantially. The small surplus suggests that receipts on US owned assets are marginally higher than payments being made. The business and investment community in general finds this very disturbing, not because receipts are lower but because increased payments mean that more and more US assets are being acquired by foreign countries. In other words, foreigners are financing most of the expenses and debt carried by the US government.

CHAPTER 9

DECLINE IN MANUFACTURING:

A discussion of US trade would be incomplete without discussing the declining manufacturing sector. It's not so much that the manufacturing market as a whole is declining; it is more that the US manufacturers have been forced to take drastic measures due to their increasing legacy costs, namely pension funds and post-retirement health care benefits coupled with union issues. At its peak Detroit was known as the automobile capital of the world. The three icons of the automotive world, General Motors, Ford and Chrysler, are based there, and working for them represented the ultimate ambition for many. The founders of these companies introduced many great ideas and technologies that continue to be successful today, but what happened to the companies?

Businesses that were once icons of this great economy are standing at the door of bankruptcy court. Why? Is it because they forgot the fundamentals of business? Or is it simply because their counterparts make better cars? GM, Chrysler and Ford cars are comparable in every aspect to their foreign counterparts. However, what they forgot was that consumer loyalties don't last forever. They forgot to move ahead with the times, and most importantly they chose to ignore one of the key principles of economics. When there is an opportunity to make profit, competition *always* finds a way to creep in.

The decade of the 1960's was the era of GM supremacy. The company established standards that others followed, and GM controlled almost half of the American car market. Today the company struggles to stay in business. What happened? When a company is as large and successful as GM arrogance comes naturally. Add to that the fact that it represented the American economy in unprecedented ways. The company had loyal customers who stayed true to the brand despite decreasing quality. Lack of good business intelligence decisions, succumbing to labor pressures, increased focus on marketing rather than product, and miscalculations of market trends cost GM its supremacy.

At this point we open the discussion to debate. What would have happened had GM not succumbed to the UAW pressures in 1998? What would have happened had it chosen to close the Flint plant rather than invest more in outmoded technology? Would the company have faced bankruptcy sooner, or would it have been another Caterpillar-like success story? These are questions to which definite answers will never be known. However, logical and rational conclusions can be drawn from lessons of the past. At the outset, it has been proven that any form of organized labor union typically will result in increased costs with degrees of change in overall productivity in the long term.

For the members of the labor union, wage benefits exist; however, free market forces are a much greater positive tool to ensure competitive labor rates than unions. Having said that, GM probably could have weathered the storm of 1998, and had it done that and played the subsequent cards correctly it would not be where it is today. Going back to the future, the 1998 strike was, and for some time to come will be, a turning point in GM's history. The 1998 strike was a very emotional one both for GM and for the UAW, not so much because the company or the employees were losing money but more because it took place in Flint.

Flint, Michigan, is where GM and the UAW have their roots. Flint is where the UAW acquired the contractual right for organized strikes through the 1936-37 sit down strike. Flint is a town that has been raised by the automotive industry, so when the same industry starts outsourcing jobs to cut costs emotions naturally run very high. Through research of different media publications it seems that the UAW was completely in favor of making GM competitive and regaining its market share, but the problems were rooted in deciding how to achieve that competitiveness.

With success also comes complacency and resistance to change. Burdened under its history of inefficiency, troubles that arose in the form of decreasing market share, outmoded technology, inflexible labor contracts, lack of focus towards quality and continued product improvement compounded the challenges GM needed to overcome in 1998. Meeting all these challenges in one shot was monumental.

GM's dependence and the UAW's stubbornness were not things that would melt away quickly. But there were multiple factors that GM could have controlled. The most important and most basic one was improved product quality and design. Subsequent to the annual meeting GM CEO Rick Waggoner conceded, "If we had a chance to rerun the last five years, we probably would have done a little more thinking about making sure that each product was distinctive and had a chance to be successful." [53]

American management is often called the myopic style of management. Short-term management achieves tactical objectives and short-term market expectations; however, focusing on the short term can obscure strategic performance and take everyone's eye off the central focus of the company. The focus, when executed correctly, almost always results in greater future earnings. Having a central focus was the prime differentiating factor in many leading companies. For some the focus was people, while for others the focus was innovative company culture.

It almost seems like GM has been blinded by all the glitter and glitz of the New Economy. It failed to see the evolving trends of globalization; it failed to see the possible trend of increasing fuel costs; and, more importantly, it failed to recognize the potential of its Japanese counterparts. GM concentrated more on finance and marketing rather than designing better products. The Old Economy bromide that "bigger is better" has been evolving to smaller and more nature-friendly products. GM failed to recognize this trend. It also missed the boat and underestimated the emerging trend of crossover vehicles, which are lighter SUV's.

While many argue that increased labor costs and post-retirement benefits have led GM to bankruptcy, research for this book indicates that these are the end results of problems that were embedded in poor management. It is not UAW's fault that people refused to buy GM cars. Having a union is quite acceptable as long as the company can continue to improve its market share and profit margins. An important tool for managing unions is proper human resource management. Unionized companies should have a lean, manageable work force and avoid over-hiring. GM failed to do this; thus, the problems at GM have been simmering for a long time. Only now have they reached the boiling point and threaten to flow over to the global economy.

GM's continued success is important for the US economy, not so much from a financial point of view as from an emotional perspective. Can you imagine America without General Motors? For its continued long-term success it is important that the company swallow the bitter pill and take a strong, firm stand against the UAW. Even a long strike is acceptable as long as GM continues to be firm and does not succumb

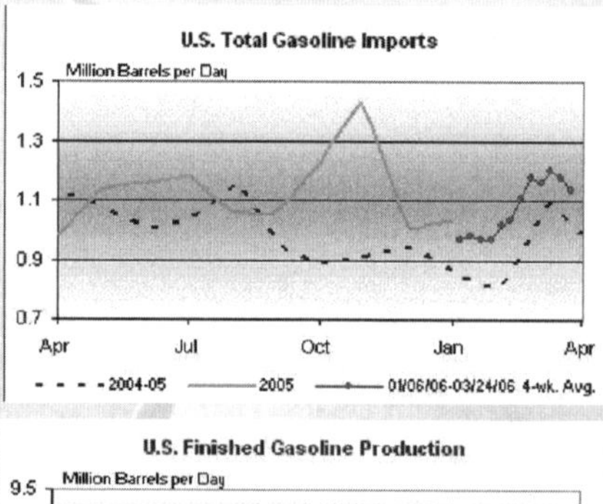

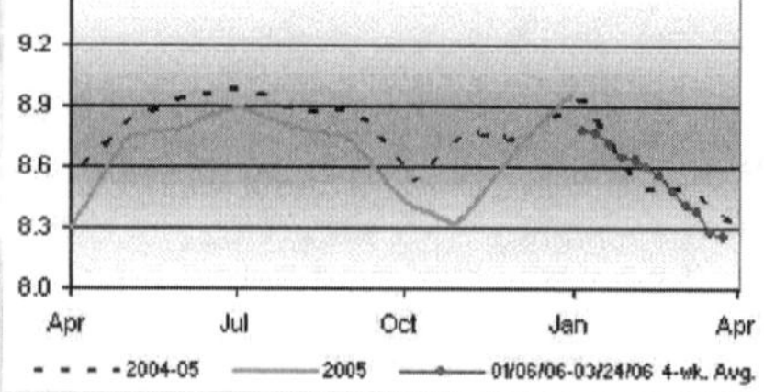

Source: www.doe.gov

to the pressures of a union again. And if GM cannot do that, then they should simply follow the airline industry and let the bankruptcy courts handle the UAW. Companies both within and outside the manufacturing sector should take lessons from GM's story, for it is a story of how a great empire can reach the brink of extinction by the seemingly small but powerful forces of free trade and a free market.

INCREASED DEPENDENCE ON PETROLEUM PRODUCTS:

Moving on, the conundrum of the New Economy only grows bigger and more interesting. See the adjacent graph obtained from the Department of Energy website. The DOE forecast of petroleum demand increases exponentially by 2030. Petroleum is a non-renewable energy resource that is mostly imported into the United States. According to the BEA's current account details, one third of the increase in goods imports can be attributed to petroleum and related products. This increase is partly due to continued increase in demand and also to the increase in the price of crude oil. Isn't it worth thinking about that when the US economy could withstand one of the largest stock market crashes and the inhumane and devastating September 11 attacks the sudden increase in oil prices poses an even bigger challenge?

While the continued increase in demand can be argued and justified by blaming it on lack of adequate public transportation, except in a few metropolitan areas, often the U.S. public transportation system is considered inferior. In other words, public transportation is a service whose demand increases in recessionary periods, and its use by an average consumer decreases on a daily basis. Even in cities where public transportation is available, such as New York, people utilize the service not because they are environment-conscious but mostly because public parking is scarce and very expensive in these cities. It is crucial to note here that this increase in demand will soon spread to the developing nations, also. As their appetite for bigger cars increases, the demand for petroleum and related products will increase, too.

This continued surge in demand, coupled with the war against terrorism and the uncertainty of world economies towards the Muslim world, exert another powerful upward force on the price of oil. Pay attention to these numbers as detailed in the *National Energy Policy Report* [54] because we can expect that the US consumption of oil will increase by thirty-two percent to 25.8 billion barrels per day by 2020, as compared against 19.5 million barrels in 2000. In analyzing previous graphs, it is clear that most of this increase will flow from foreign countries or through imports. Clearly US production is on the decline, while the imports are on the rise. With the increase in the current account deficit already at an alarming level and economic growth expected to slow down, can the US continue to increase its dependence on foreign oil reserves? Noteworthy is the fact that *in addition to supplying credit and funding its debt, foreign countries are also the source of our energy supply.*

NATURAL DISASTERS: MOTHER NATURE TAKING CONTROL:

Increases in the consumption of petroleum or any non-renewable energy resource will inevitably be accompanied by an increase in pollution. The obvious sources of pollution are automobiles and industrial factories. Less known is the fact that the lack of responsible behavior by society is the largest contributor to pollution. The subject of industrial pollution is well-known and hotly debated. The recent debacle of the energy giant Enron is an example of how individuals can benefit at the cost of society.

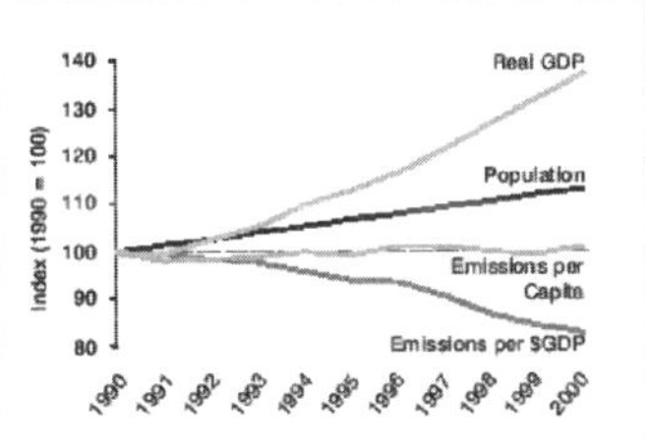

Source: BEA (2001), U.S. Census Bureau (2000), and emission estimates in this report.

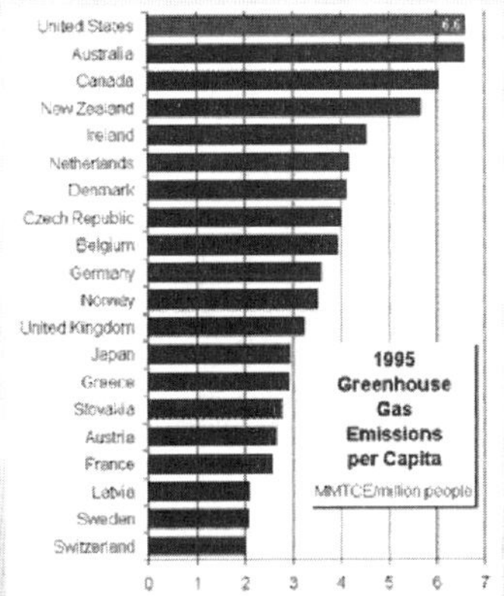

Source: www.epa.gov

Global warming is a subject we have all studied at some level during our education. We are all familiar with the greenhouse effect diagram and how the emissions of greenhouse gases, such as carbon dioxide, are deteriorating our environment in unprecedented ways. El Niño, the Tsunami of 2004, and Hurricane Katrina of 2005 are examples of Mother Nature giving us warning signs and hoping to draw our attention to the planet Earth. According to the National Academy of Sciences the earth's temperature has risen by one degree Fahrenheit in the past century. A one-degree change in temperature for a household means nothing; but when the same one-degree change happens on a global level and causes increased melting of glaciers, which in turn cause the sea level to rise and thus erode land, the effects can be quite devastating. Naturally carbon dioxide is a byproduct of all green vegetation, but before the industrialization of earth began the carbon dioxide level in the atmosphere was fairly static, and the earth's temperature varied around an average of sixty degrees Fahrenheit.

As industrialization began and man began to burn more fossil fuels to generate electricity and operate automobiles, the balance was disturbed, and we are now emitting more than the natural atmosphere can absorb. The end result is that the earth's temperature is rising because greenhouse gases are heat-trapping gases. The EPA website presents some interesting facts on US emissions compared to other countries. It is no surprise that, on a per capita basis, the US takes the first spot.

Scientists expect that global temperatures could rise anywhere from one to four and one-half degrees Fahrenheit in the next fifty years. To add to the problem, while weather models can provide estimates they cannot provide accurate answers to regional variability. Predicting the increase or decrease in regional precipitation and its consequence on inhabitants and vegetation is beyond the scope of any computer model. All predictions are surrounded by an array of ifs and buts.

How does all this influence the New Economy? Think of Hurricane Katrina in 2005 and think of the Tsunami of late 2004. Hurricane Katrina virtually destroyed the city of New Orleans and with it a significant percentage of US petroleum refining capability, which in turn created fear and uncertainty in the world oil market, ultimately affecting the US stock market. Surprisingly, the US economy absorbed the shock very well. Part of the explanation for our relatively painless recovery was the financial engineering that enabled a soft landing, but another important factor was the increasing proximity between countries which allowed them to lend a helping hand during our time of acute need. The helping-hand in such risk management situations is often in the form of financial aid.

As the people of United States and, more importantly, as inhabitants of this great planet, we need to remember that no resource is indefinite. Mother Nature can only give us so much, and she has already sustained us for the thousands of years we have lived here. As the developing countries evolve toward the US model of industrialization they will continue to use more resources, and in the process they will deplete more of our finite resources at an accelerated rate. As China and India move ahead in their quest to become the economies of the 21st century, their consumption levels will increase at the same rate as the United States. Also bear in mind their populations are many times the size of ours.

The explosion of the automobile market, the increase in manufacturing trends, and the upward trend of American fast food will only add to more pollution. Within the US, when we talk of past increases in oil prices and the future expected increases we often think about the hostile and unstable political relations of America with the Middle East or the Muslim world in general. We forget to take into account the changing economic situation across the globe. It is easy to forget that with industrialization comes increased demand for power.

A case in point is China, which is now growing at an annual rate of eight percent and is expected to grow at even faster pace. [55] To enable such growth, China is not only rapidly consuming its own reserves of coal it is also relying heavily on imported oil and gas. And in order to ensure continued supply, China is developing positive relationships with countries that have oil but are not as positively disposed toward the US. In doing so, the future of the US-China partnership does come into question. Furthermore, policies and agreements developed earlier continue to recognize China and India as developing countries, in turn granting them many exemptions. For example, under the Kyoto protocol China is initially exempt from carbon emissions penalties, and the reality is that today China has the second largest emissions for carbon dioxide. [56] Shouldn't these protocols be revised to reflect the current and true situation of the countries?

One may argue that changing things at national levels is a cumbersome task, surrounded by politics and the protocol that follows it. So let's focus our attention on individuals such as you and me, so that small incremental changes multiplied across hundreds of millions of people can make a huge difference to the state of our planet. Of course, we can make a difference! The EPA website at **www.epa.gov** has a list of DIY tasks that can, in small steps, help us to improve our environment. While the literature is there, often the motivation is what is lacking. There is an immense need for a change of attitude. It is important for individuals to realize that while buying a Ford Expedition is fun, it is also equivalent to consciously ignoring the demand of nature and the times. The need today is for smaller, more efficient cars, not big gas hogs. The same is true for houses. Palatial houses are comfortable, but do we really need them? Does it have to take exorbitant real estate prices for us to rethink and evaluate our needs and wants?

We are a society of "everything big:" big houses, big cars, bigger meals, and with all that, bigger egos, too. Unlike today, when every evening we see our neighbors drive into their garage, and the best source of entertainment available for the children is the television set, even in the US there was a time when children enjoyed playing on the streets and neighbors fed each other. When and how did we change? Did success feed our egos, making us arrogant? Or did we simply get so busy in trying to satisfy the ever-increasing needs that we forgot the importance of saying hello to our neighbors?

THE US SOCIETY – LOST, AND FINDING ITS WAY

We now discuss the last but the most important aspect of the New Economy: people and society. American society and culture has been and continues to be a trendsetter. It is often used as a synonym for the entire Western society. This is contradictory because America as a country is very young compared to many of its European counterparts. Going back to history, America has in some ways evolved from its European counterparts. Therefore, calling it synonymous to the Western culture is only a complement to the US. From its discovery in 1492 by Christopher Columbus to the present day, America has evolved into a melting pot of different cultures. Immigrants from all parts of the world have come here in hope of freedom and a better life, and for they most part they have achieved them. The assimilation of different cultures has been one of the greatest boons to this country. With different cultures come varied perspectives and ideologies, and just as anything else in nature,only the best values survive and thrive.

The blending of different cultures or the influx of individuals into a foreign unknown land has, over time, also set the tone of the society. The Eastern world has often criticized the US's individualistic way of living. Is this something we chose? Or was it more a matter of situational learning that led us this way? This is not a historical treatise, but with the utmost humility and with all due respect to the great thinkers it seems that a lot of it was situational learning. At this point it is important to remember that the US has been a big melting pot for different nationalities and still continues to be one. Individuals from different walks of life and nationalities have come to America, hoping to find a better life for themselves and future generations, and most of them have succeeded. This blending of different nationalities also brought with it the "watch out for yourself" attitude.

As immigrants came into this foreign land they both threatened and were threatened by the natives. Taking care of oneself was a necessity for survival. Over time this evolved into what is now called American culture, which in the Eastern world is often considered cold and unemotional. Capitalism, in some ways, is a natural by-product of individualism. What is capitalism? The exact definition can have varied forms, but fundamentally speaking it is a system where individuals who trade for profit control the factors of production.

In the settling days, when the formal business entity did not exist, individuals traded in commodities that they wanted, and as trade evolved a more formal medium of exchange, money, came into existence. The connection between individualism and capitalism is obvious. When individuals own resources, they will naturally trade for profit only. Unlike other continents, the US has never seen socialism as a way of living. For a very long time economists have argued the benefits of one versus the other. Both systems have pros and cons. While socialism cannot work in today's free world, one can see why the system would be preferred one hundred years ago for many countries. Just as poverty, increasing inflation, and increasing unemployment are the disadvantages of a socialist society, materialism, arrogance, and complacency are the disadvantages of a successful capitalistic model. Additionally, in a society where nationalities intermingle reception to change is always much higher. Just like people, countries have an age cycle, too. Older countries tend to be more steadfast in attitudes and less likely to respond to changing times. The US as a country has always adapted to change very quickly, and this allowed it to be an extremely productive country that recognized changing patterns since its discovery. *Through most of the twentieth century this country has given businesses the policies and freedom to invent and produce commodities that were required by not only its citizens but also by citizens of the world.*

How is it that a country considered to be **the** superpower, whose currency dominates the global financial market, and whose acceptance has been and continues to be sought after by politicians and businessmen alike, suddenly comes under the intense criticism of spreading its imperialism and eroding the ethnic values systems of other foreign lands? Why is it that a high school student in India or China knows more about the US than a graduate in the US knows about India or China? Why is it that, until recently, media in the US has been ethnocentric and very rarely focuses on the positive aspects of other cultures? Quite honestly, at the lowest level of society it is ignorance that continues to exist due to arrogance at the higher level of the society.

Remember our discussion regarding GM? With success comes complacency and a "can't touch me" attitude. The same is true for the upper level of society. We are not talking of economic divides here but rather the levels in America that include the government and the media. The onus of educating the public rests on the shoulders of both the media and the education system. The responsibility of designing an educational system that allows its students to have a global perspective and skill set lies on the shoulders of the state and federal governments and the local boards of education.

The recent wave of off-shoring has left many Americans angry and frustrated. American businesses have been roundly criticized by other Americans for sending "American jobs" to third-world countries to save costs. The solution to this is simple: the fundamental education system.

There are some stark differences in the American education system in contrast to, say, the Asian education system. For example, let's focus on the Asian subcontinent of India since India represents the largest democracy in the region and has the highest pool of educated English-speaking workers. The Indian education system emphasizes mathematics and science, the two subjects that instill the process of logical reasoning and rationalization. The emphasis is so important that students are not allowed to use calculators, even in high school. Even for complex calculus problems the students use manual logarithm tables and formulas they must think through. This does not discount that the American education system does not produce mathematics wizards or scientists. However, the percentage is significantly less. *There is a reason why Asian and Chinese students dominate most engineering and science graduate level programs.* One of the greatest strengths of the American education system is its flexibility and reward. It has flexibility because students can choose from a variety of subjects that interest them and that meet their credit requirements for a course. The reward is that, in the US, a conscious attempt is made to not hurt a student's self-esteem. While these attributes are important at fostering an overall, knowledgeable, confident student, such an emphasis also reduces the student's chance to excel in the larger world.

Flexibility allows students to avoid subjects that are hard and demanding in favor of easier subjects that allow them to meet credit requirements. The reward pattern encourages confidence and self-esteem, but it doesn't push students to seek any higher intellectual attainment. In contrast, students in India and China are constantly drilled both at home and at school to improve their performance on problems of logic and science. Again, both systems have their merits and drawbacks. If the Asian system produces better software engineers, the American system produces better marketers and public speakers. If the Asian system emphasizes math and science, the American system allows individuals to express themselves, generally resulting in higher and better communication skills.

Until recently this was acceptable, but with the changing economic patterns and the increase in labor supply in the form of global labor, the American education system is proving to be at a disadvantage. Not because the core fundamentals are not taught, but because the emphasis has come too late. Capitalism within an education system will automatically translate to higher costs for everyone. Thanks to the credit society and the concept of privacy being so strong, individuals are eager to work early and live independently. Consequently not all attend college, and most are happy with an hourly job that pays the bills. With the hourly wage paying jobs now transferred to nations across domestic borders, these individuals are now left with a skill set that is obsolete. This is where the government (not to mention the education system) must step in to give a helping hand and create opportunities in the New Economy to allow adults to upgrade their skills. Does anyone wonder what the significant advantages are of spending only a fraction of the tax dollars on credits to universities for offering subsidized programs for workers laid off within their states? With the extent of freedom available to the US media, it is amazing and perplexing how ethnocentric the media is. A typical CNN newscast, until recently, very rarely talked about anything but US issues. Why? Nations across the globe have been dealing with terrorism for a very long time. So why is it that it took the horrifying tragedy of 9/11 for us to awaken to the cries of those nations? And, once awakened, why and how are we continuing to alienate ourselves from the rest of the world?

The fight against terrorism is a global fight, but doesn't it seem like it has become our fight while the rest of the world deals with the seemingly less important issues of globalization and competing in the New Economy? These are complex questions the answers to which are more emotional and less logical. However, one thing is clear. Had the media and the education system in the US been more global, the average citizen and, consequently, businesses would have been better prepared for the wave of globalization. If we were able to provide affordable and appropriate education, wouldn't many more children have had a college education and a better skill set to adapt themselves to these emerging changes? Had we not been so arrogant, ignorant, and blinded by our "success" we could have seen competition coming from other parts of the world. Had our demands not gone beyond the norms we could have avoided being labeled as a credit society. Had we paid a little more attention to the declining birth rate and the fact that very soon the majority of the work force will retire we would have made better decisions on healthcare and maybe even created opportunities for those individuals to continue to work.

When we know and understand the above results, why is it that we have not been able to prevent them from happening? None of the dilemmas above have a black and white solution. They are extremely complex problems entwined within both the national and global economy.

"ECONOMY:" ENTITY OR CONCEPT?

"Economy" is a word heard in settings as varied as elementary classrooms and corporate boardrooms. What is economy? Is it simply the balance of assets versus liabilities of the country? Or does it also take into account the state of the individual, both financial and emotional? Unfortunately, academic definitions of economy focus on the production, distribution, and consumption of wealth. Defining economy in this manner would be acceptable if the only factor influencing the citizens of a country was the distribution of wealth. Research consistently shows, however, that this is not so. For if it were so the citizens of the United States would be the happiest individuals, while citizens of developing or third world countries would be the unhappiest. This is not what we find.

The 2004 Swedish-based World Happiness Survey, which is conducted every four years, ranked the US fifteenth while several South American countries shared the first spot. [57] Is it time for us as a leading economic power to change the measure of success? GDP and its expected growth are often cited as ***the*** economic success measure. Is it time to introduce a measure that includes "happiness" in this? Would it be prudent for the world's leading power to take clues from the far smaller and poorer country of [58] Bhutan, which measures its growth by Gross National Happiness (GNH)? The fundamental problem is that the economy that we talk of does not exist in isolation and is not something that can be defined by a simple mathematical formula with certain underlying economic assumptions. The economy in today's world is an entity, an entity that is unique to every country; and just like individuals, all economic entities have their own personality traits.

While the concept of this new paradigm does exist, the implementation is yet to come. A fundamental yet very important principle in economics is cash-flow of a society. The concept is simple: the households supply the resources of production, which are used by business to generate goods and services that are in turn used by households again. Hence the cycle of cash flow in a society completes itself. If we extend this to include the government, financial institutions, and other business entities we can see correlations, such as the way an increase in interest rates can influence the economy as a whole.

We use the example of a university, but we can substitute any government area of control such as schools, public transportation, and infrastructure to understand the implications. Let's take the example of building a new university campus. Of course, some universities are private, but they have their share of government support. For starters, just the initiation will require a huge amount of funding that in addition to donations will come from the credit market.

Businesses and government alike borrow from the credit market. The inflow or supply of money to the credit market comes from household savings, both national and global. The task of building a university will require inflow and outflow of resources to and from businesses. The factors of production in the form of labor arise, once again, from households; in turn, the households receive wages and other benefits from businesses. Once completed, the university provides valuable resources to businesses, to individuals and to government.

The source of revenue for the university is tuition it collects which, again, is often funded by the credit market. The university, in turn, imparts knowledge to the students and prepares them to enter the work force. For businesses and government the university provides insightful research and analysis on the strategic challenges they face. Let's assume for a moment that our society is in complete balance and that there are no surprise elements. In such a situation it is a "win-win" for all, and things progress smoothly.

To this let's add the twist of an increase in interest rates. What happens? Theoretically, the households anticipating inflation save more. The cost of borrowing increases for businesses, government, and the university as well.. This drives up costs.. To offset that cost increase the university might increase its fee structure, and so on. When costs increase employers look for ways to reduce their fixed expenses, and this frequently means cutting staff. So when we add the additional wave of layoffs then joblessness increases and spending is thereby reduced. As individual incomes decrease people have less to spend on education, and many students stay away from expensive colleges and choose community colleges that at best prepare them for routine hourly jobs. There are countless twists we can apply to this example, and the results will vary accordingly. The idea behind introducing this example was not to take you through all of the twists and turns in an economy but to simply drive home the point that the economy in today's world is not as isolated as many people might think.

No country in the present world can live in isolation, even if it wants to. When decisions are made with an isolationist mentality they are often detrimental. Nations are in a very strong symbiotic relationship with each other today. The sooner they realize this the better their chances of succeeding in the New Economy.

We all saw the future come "one day at a time," and yet we chose to ignore the warning signs. Why? When the Internet bubble burst, why were we surprised? Analysts warned us of the inflated numbers. The Federal Reserve raised cautions and advisories against unnatural increases. Today we are being warned of the housing bubble, and we continue to ignore it and to borrow even more based on speculative wealth. Fundamental principles of accounting and finance have taught us that companies with negative cash flow cannot and should not have a high "price to earnings ratio" (P/E ratio) unless the company can demonstrate actual returns. Yet we borrow heavily for real estate in the blind belief that its value will always go up and never go down, which makes us look wealthy on paper but also puts us at tremendous risk.

How is it that our nation which once produced enough to feed not only our own citizens but also the citizens of other countries now depends on those very countries to feed ourselves? The only logical answer is continued change in the direction of decreasing supply (needs) and increasing demand (wants). Needs are basic items required for survival: food, clothes and shelter. Wants are luxury items that are not needed but can make life easier. For example, five years ago cellular phones were "wants" for many, but today many people view them as a "need." (There is a saying in the business discipline of marketing: A luxury once experienced becomes a necessity.) How many of us have actually turned around and returned home because we forgot our cell phone and yet vividly remember a time when we did not own one?

The itemization of needs versus wants is relative. Needs of a developed nation are wants in the developing world. As the continuum between wants and needs shortens, the society in general has to work harder to satisfy demand. This growing appetite for more creates a circle, a circle that demands higher working efficiencies and increased earnings. The want of more money often leads us to self-destructive games.

Money, though merely a concept, is often treated as an actual commodity. Many transactions happen across the globe and no money, per se, changes hands. Trade happens by simple debit and credit entries in a ledger. The recent trend of share buybacks and the returning popularity of mergers and acquisitions have created stirs in the financial markets. This, true to the myopic American management style, is a short-term strategy which is making the stockholders happy and the bondholders extremely cautious.

True to the multiple quandaries of the New Economy, this dilemma is also unique. On one hand we have a manufacturing sector strapped for cash, and on the other hand we have companies buying back shares to return some of the value to their shareholders. When a company returns cash it is telling the market that none of the future projects can provide good returns. Is this really true? Shouldn't the companies prepare themselves for the expected slowdown? Health care costs are increasing; can't employers use cash surpluses to provide better and continued health care to its existing employees? With manufacturing on a downturn, why not reinvest in it to revive this crucial economic sector?

It's amazing to see that in spite of all the lessons that we learned in the beginning of the 21st century we still fail to see that the US is no longer the only power in the world. The world has grown very small, and other countries that once depended on us are now not only financing us but also providing us the essentials of life. We have read the numerous reports that tout the fact that China will dominate the first half of this century and that India will be a close second. What about Singapore or Dubai? Both countries have been investing large sums of money in their respective technical and social infrastructures. The UK has enjoyed tremendous growth and is poised to continue for the next several years. The European Union continues to expand with many new members from the former "eastern bloc" and will soon equal the buying power and influence of the United States. The future will be significantly more global and competitive in every way.

AT&T is a case in point. In the famous "divestiture decision" of 1984, Bell Telephone was split into seven RBOC's (Regional Bell Operating Companies), known as Baby Bells, to stimulate innovation and competition, with the original AT&T essentially becoming a long-distance telephone company with its own laboratory. However the Baby Bells once again are merging under the umbrella of AT&T driven by the threat of competition.

Arvind Virmani (Director, Indian Council for Research on International Economic Relations) has proposed the idea of a tri-polar world compared with the past uni-polar world dominated by the United States. Through research he basically presents the idea that China, India, and the US will form a "Holy Trinity." While the numbers and theory might support such a change, real life raises objections. For starters the power and influence of the European members would prevent such a theory from becoming a reality; and other resource-rich countries, such as Australia, Canada, Denmark, Venezuela, Saudi Arabia, South Africa et al, would resist such a development, especially considering that China and India are, even today, more rivals than neighbors. [59]

Nevertheless, considering the increasing trend of Asian economies influencing the global economy it is sad to see the sustained arrogance of the US governance. It is time the media provide a true picture of the US economy, a picture that has increased levels of debt, a picture that shows the true dependence on petroleum products, a picture that shows the increasing healthcare costs alongside the increasing number of retirees, and a *picture that presents the US as part of the world and not as the world itself.*

Elaine Maxwell said, "My will shall shape the future. Whether I fail or succeed shall be no man's doing but my own. I am the force; I can clear any obstacle before me or I can be lost in the maze. My choice; my responsibility; win or lose, only I hold the key to my destiny." It is true the people of the United States hold the keys to the success of this great country. Their decisions to concentrate on the economy, healthcare, the Federal deficit, global warming, education, employment, Afghanistan, or Iraq will decide the economic scenario in the current and coming years. Their choice of who will lead and represent this country will decide the continued or discontinued dominance of America as the world's leading power.

The New Economy is an economy of paradoxes. The success of this economy and our country lies in balancing the seesaw of economic, political and social principles.

The upcoming chapter discusses the dramatic changes taking place in the country and what has the potential to become the end of America as we know it today. It will argue that to save the America we know will require major and radically different policies on education, healthcare, poverty, employment, global warming, and foreign relations.

CHAPTER 10

The End of America as We Know It?

"The true beginning of our end."

– William Shakespeare,
A Midsummer Night's Dream

CHAPTER 10

History repeats itself, we all know. But do we all believe it? Do we remember to learn from the lessons of the past? The United States could have learned a great deal from both the UK and Russia based on their respective adventures in and occupations of Iraq and Afghanistan, for example. It's ironic, but often the best practices arise from what we learn by watching others apply the worst practices, and it is possible to learn lessons of great value even from the creative world of art and literature.

Caesar once established himself as the greatest politician in Rome. He accomplished everything he wanted to do. He had triumphed over all his opponents, and he had no equals. His defeat came at the hands of his own supporters. This is *"the true beginning of our end."* Consider yourself warned. Ironically, the signs of caution are appearing at the same time as the US is still basking in the glory and the belief of being the "supreme world power."

The Internet literally introduced us to a new dimension, the fourth dimension, one that encourages us to be creative, imaginative, and one that throws caution to the wind. The same e-era that created vast wealth for many and saw the largest economic expansion in the history of our country unfortunately also laid the framework for the majority of the global issues we face today.

So far our discussion has centered on identifying the key elements of changing business and social paradigms. Now we will try to link all the individual pieces together to form the bigger picture, a picture that is sad, that is scary and, if not re-drawn correctly, that can alter the face of our world in the span of our own lives. As we connect the pieces and find the missing links, you will see how the dissimilar and seemingly unimportant issues of preserving the environment, minimizing the energy crisis, reforming education, and coping with the changing social environment can influence our wel-being in unprecedented ways.

The prime question facing our nation today is, "How can we make the types of radical changes needed for our long term growth and survival?

COSTS OF WAR:

The horrifying events of September 11, 2001, made the world aware of the hatred some harbored for America and the western world. While other nations across the globe have dealt with comparatively primitive forms of terrorism for years, 9/11 was a wake-up call to the United States to fight terrorism collectively. However, what started off as the world's united effort has evolved into a unilateral campaign by President George W. Bush to combat terrorism and, according to some, has catalyzed a worldwide movement of Islamic extremism. His decision to invade Iraq as an element in the "war on terror" has proven to be expensive. The cost of the Iraq war as of January 2007 exceeds $358 billion dollars! (Those interested in the dollar cost of the Iraq war to date can find it at www.nationalpriorities.org.)

It is interesting that the US Government spends almost thirty percent of income taxes on the military, alone. It spends only 4.1% on education and a whopping nineteen percent in interest on the federal deficit. Veterans' benefits from the prior wars are 3.7%. With the many issues described in this book this looks like a good time to reexamine our national priorities.

America has now been at war for almost half a decade. This war has led to increased financial and budgetary pressures on the government. The current government has two important agendas: to fight terrorism and to reduce taxes. Pursuing both at the same time takes the budget in opposite directions.

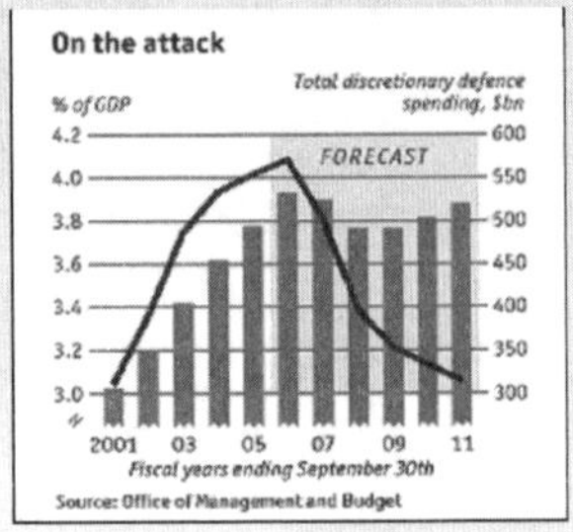

Cutting taxes implies reduced revenue for the government, and increased defense spending implies increased expenditures. How big is the increase in defense spending? The cost of war in Afghanistan and Iraq combined has increased from $306 billion to $524 billion. However, this number may be underestimated because the requests and appropriations of funds for the war are being handled on a piecemeal basis. The National Priorities Project (**www.npp.org**) estimates that fifty-six percent of the 2007 discretionary budget will be spent on defense, and other categories such as education and the environment will be allocated eight and three percent, respectively.[60]

Discretionary spending is essentially the amount on which Congress decides. The rest of the budget is mandatory spending. If fifty-six percent of the current administration's budget dollars are going to be spent on defense, what does that leave for the myriad other issues ranging from interest on debt, to education, to improving our environment? To put these numbers in a global perspective, the NPP estimates that the United States spends as much on military as the rest of the world combined! In other words, out of the total number of dollars spent on "the military" the United States takes forty-seven percent of the share, NATO allies take twenty-three percent, while Libya, Iran, Cuba, Sudan, and Syria contribute one percent. The rest of the world completes the remaining twenty-nine percent. It's interesting to note that the supposed "axis of evil" nations account for only one-percent of the total spending.

From an American perspective this might be a good thing. Increased military spending should mean an increasingly secure nation. Unfortunately the equation is not that direct. The national security of America depends not just on a strong military but also on the preventive measures we take to establish constructive relations internationally. It also depends on the Department of Homeland Security which, in addition to securing our ports, is also responsible for responding to natural and man-made emergencies. The current situation heavily favors the military. In fact, almost the entire national security budget of the United States is spent on the armed forces, leaving very little for all the other categories. [61]

The only cuts we may see are same ones we see in the business world: reductions in personnel. However, this will only increase the pressures on the troops at war. Additionally, under the most recent Quadrennial Defense Review (QDR) former Secretary of Defense Donald Rumsfeld predicted another two decades of threats to America. [62] *If so, how do we respond? It forces us to consider other ways to win peace and stability for our country besides going to war.* The sad and menacing reality of life is that terrorism has no end. The bottom line is, how do you scare or deter someone who is not afraid of death? The death of Abu Musab al-Zarqawi, al-Qaeda's leader in Iraq, is a case in point. For a moment this seemed like a victory over terrorists, but the war is far from over for both America and Iraq. Zarqawi is no more; however, he had followers who will retaliate for his death, who will continue to flourish without him, who will, sooner or later, appoint another leader to continue the vicious circle of death. A handful of extremists will always exist, and if Mr. Rumsfeld's predictions are even marginally accurate America is going to be at war far into the foreseeable future!

The financial cost of this war and the catastrophic loss of young lives will be borne by the American people for a long time

For America, that means sorrow and further increases in the already soaring foreign debt and record deficits.

LACK OF FISCAL DISCIPLINE:

Before we take an in-depth look into what the 2007 proposed budget has to offer, the previous chart (Budget FY 2007, Analytical Perspectives) shows us the main sources of revenue and costs for the government. The tables listed are the respective tables in the document available at **www.whitehouse.gov.** Just as in any other business, when the outlays exceed receipts we have a deficit. Having said that, it is also important to remember that while government assets and investment classes take into account its debt liabilities, many times the government undertakes deficit spending, in addition to spending on projects that benefit the nation as a whole, and does not necessarily improve its balance sheet.

The 2007 Budget Analytical Perspective says current policy is:

An Unsustainable Path

> *"These long-run budget projections show clearly that the budget is on an unsustainable path, although the rise in the deficit unfolds gradually. The budget deficit is projected to decline as the economy expands over the next several years, while most of the baby boomers are still in the work force. As the baby boomers begin to reach retirement age in large numbers, the deficit begins to rise. In about ten years, the deficit as a share of GDP is projected to reach a low point*

and then begin an inexorable increase. Without reforms, by the end of this chapter's projection period in 2080, rising deficits would have driven publicly held Federal debt to levels well above the previous peak level relative to GDP reached at the end of World War II. Long before that point is ever reached there is likely to be a crisis that will force budgetary changes, but the timing of the crisis and its resolution are impossible to predict." [63]

According to the OMB, federal assets are currently estimated to be seventy-seven percent higher than in 1960; whereas liabilities have increased by 244% in real terms.

RECEIPTS THROUGH APRIL
(Billions of dollars)

Major Source	Actual FY2005	Preliminary FY2006	Percentage Change
Individual Income	547	603	10.2
Corporate Income	134	174	29.5
Social Insurance	449	482	7.2
Other	86	95	10.8
Total	1,217	1,353	11.2

Sources: Department of the Treasury; CBO.

OUTLAYS THROUGH APRIL
(Billions of dollars)

Major Category	Actual FY2005	Preliminary FY2006	Percentage Change: Actual	Percentage Change: Adjusted[a]
Defense—Military	273	286	5.1	6.4
Social Security Benefits	297	314	5.8	5.8
Medicare	191	209	9.2	13.7
Medicaid	105	103	-1.8	-1.8
Other Programs and Activities	483	496	2.5	5.7
Subtotal	1,349	1,408	4.4	6.4
Net Interest on the Public Debt	105	129	23.2	23.2
Total	1,454	1,537	5.7	7.6

Sources: Department of the Treasury; CBO.

a. Excludes the effects of payments that were shifted because of weekends, holidays, or changes in the accounting of certain health payments of the Department of Defense.

This wide difference has led to excess liabilities of approximately $5.7 trillion, averaging to about $20,000 per capita. In GDP terms, the deficit, which was about fifty-two percent of GDP and that had declined to about thirty-eight percent in 2000, now stands at about 45% in 2005.

According to the May 2006 numbers, the Congressional Budget Office estimates the federal government deficit for FY 2006 to be close to $300 billion, and the preliminary estimates for

FY 2006 reaffirm the initial conclusion of continued increases in military spending. Also notice the increased payment of interest on public debt compared to FY 2005.

What does this mean for the average middle class family? Admittedly the 2.3% deficit (of GDP), as projected in the May numbers, is still below the historical high of 4.3% (1982-1993); but this is still higher than the overall average of 1.2% and considerably higher than the 0.1% during the Clinton administration. [64] Furthermore, when we project the increased levels of debt against GDP the current numbers are a positive 4.4% compared against a -16.4% during 1993-2001. Add to this the strong balance sheets of all major corporations. When corporations are flush with excess cash, and in many situations returning the excess cash to their stockholders as dividends, why is the government running such excessive levels of debt?

Furthermore, as we studied the long-term projections in the FY 2006 Analytical Perspectives versus FY 2007 Analytical Perspectives the situation became even more interesting. The projections have changed dramatically in one year. The FY 2006 projects in five-year increments whereas the FY 2007 projection is in ten-year increments. That is quite a stretch. Even the most successful enterprises don't make ten year plans.

In times when the world is changing everyday, projecting accurately for ten years is quite meaningless. Furthermore, the deficit projections for 2075 in 2006 were close to eighteen percent of GDP. For FY 2007 the deficit projection is between 6.9% and 13%. While the difference is significant, there is no rationale given in the analysis for the change. At this point it is important to restate that the federal deficit should not be confused with current account and trade deficit. These economic indicators were discussed at length in the preceding section, and, to summarize, based 2005 numbers the US is running a current account deficit at 6.4% of GDP.

For example, examine the government's own long term projections as presented in the 2006 budget. The 2005 deficit runs at 3.5% of GDP, and while the government claims it will cut the deficit in half before the end of this decade its projections don't reveal the same story. The deficit, if anything, is only increasing and rises to 2.7% by 2025, once again higher than the overall average of 1.2%. Subsequent to 2025 the increase in the deficit is almost exponential, reaching 18.4% by 2075.

It could be argued that the economy has improved, and hence the numbers presented under the 2007 budget are significantly different. Even if this were true, the projections are well below respective averages and call for a cautious approach. Nevertheless, the point of presenting the multiple tables and numbers is to bring home the point that the government debt, current account and trade deficits are all in the red. Corrective measures need to be taken today.

TABLE 1: FY 2006 LONG RANGE BUDGET PROJECTIONS.

2006 LONG-RANGE MODEL RESULTS

(As a percent of GDP)

	1995	2005	2015	2025	2035	2045	2055	2065	2075
Receipts	18.5	16.8	18.5	19.1	19.6	20.2	20.9	21.5	22.0
Outlays:									
Discretionary	7.4	7.9	5.9	5.9	5.9	5.9	5.9	5.9	5.9
Mandatory:									
Social Security	4.5	4.2	4.4	5.4	6.0	6.0	6.1	6.2	6.4
Medicare	2.1	2.4	3.3	4.6	6.0	7.0	7.9	9.1	10.4
Medicaid	1.2	1.5	1.9	2.1	2.3	2.6	2.8	3.0	3.3
Other	2.2	2.8	2.0	1.7	1.5	1.3	1.2	1.1	1.0
Subtotal, mandatory	10.1	10.9	11.6	13.8	15.8	16.9	18.0	19.5	21.2
Net Interest	3.2	1.5	1.9	2.0	3.1	4.9	6.9	9.7	13.3
Total outlays	20.7	20.3	19.4	21.8	24.8	27.6	30.8	35.1	40.4
Surplus or Deficit (–)	–2.2	–3.5	–0.9	–2.7	–5.2	–7.4	–10.0	–13.6	–18.4
Federal Debt Held by the Public	49.2	38.6	35.6	38.1	58.7	90.4	130.0	181.3	249.0

www.whitehouse.gov

Source: Analytical Perspectives, FY 2006 p. ---- (www.whitehouse.gov)

TABLE 2: FY 2007 LONG RUN BUDGET PROJECTIONS.

2007 LONG-RUN BUDGET PROJECTIONS

(receipts, outlays, surplus or deficit, and debt as a percent of GDP)

	1980	1990	2000	2010	2020	2030	2040	2060	2080
Receipts	19.0	18.0	20.9	17.9	18.9	19.4	20.0	21.3	22.4
Outlays:									
Discretionary	10.1	8.7	6.3	6.1	5.6	5.6	5.6	5.6	5.6
Mandatory:									
Social Security	4.3	4.3	4.2	4.2	4.9	5.8	5.9	6.1	6.4
Medicare	1.1	1.7	2.0	2.8	3.7	5.0	6.1	7.9	10.4
Medicaid	0.5	0.7	1.2	1.5	1.9	2.1	2.3	2.8	3.3
Other	3.7	3.2	2.4	2.3	1.9	1.6	1.4	1.1	0.9
Subtotal, mandatory	9.6	9.9	9.8	10.8	12.4	14.4	15.7	17.8	21.0
Net Interest	1.9	3.2	2.3	1.9	1.4	1.5	2.3	4.7	9.4
Total outlays	21.7	21.8	18.4	18.9	19.4	21.6	23.6	28.2	36.1
Surplus or Deficit (–)	–2.7	–3.9	2.4	–1.0	–0.6	–2.2	–3.6	–6.9	–13.7
Primary Surplus or Deficit (–)	–0.8	–0.6	4.7	0.9	0.9	–0.6	–1.3	–2.1	–4.2
Federal Debt Held by the Public	26.1	42.0	35.1	37.5	26.2	28.8	43.3	98.6	177.4

www.whitehouse.gov

Source: Analytical Perspectives, FY 2007 (www.whitehouse.gov)

Add to this federal deficit the savings deficit to be faced soon, and the future suddenly looks heavily mortgaged.

THE AGING WORLD:

Declining birthrates and increased life spans are two opposite sides of the continuum of life. Typically, nations have always tipped on one side or the other, and very rarely do you see a nation with the perfect population. While Asia faces the problem of over-population and thus excess employable individuals, the US faces the problem of under-population, which is partly improved by continued immigration. China, on the other hand, has made an attempt to control the population explosion through legal barriers to both immigration and the number of children allowed per family, but their cultural preference for male children means many men in China won't find mates.

Aging in any country poses a couple of unique problems. First, an aging population translates to a reduced labor force. Second, aging reduces household savings. As individuals retire they begin withdrawing from their savings to sustain their lifestyles. Additionally, their contributions toward income taxes and other government funds such as social security are eliminated, thus reducing the revenues for government. Last but not least, the increased healthcare demands of the elderly put further pressure on government budgets.

According to the MGI (McKinsey Global Institute) report, unless there is a dramatic change in the savings pattern of the present working class the aging process across the globe will cause a shortfall of $31 trillion by 2024. Across the various countries, the United States contributes the largest shortfall of $19 trillion; this is followed by Japan, which is contributing a shortfall of $8 trillion. Many believe that the shortfall can be offset by increased borrowing. This is often suggested based on the premise that global trade and robust economies have allowed countries to help financially across borders.

While this is true, it is important to remember that other successful economies will offer financial aid only if the savings rate in their countries is positive. Many successful economies, including the UK and Japan, are seeing reduced savings ratios. To put things in perspective, America's savings today are less than one percent of our income, compared to seven percent in the 1990's. Compared to the savings rate in the 1990s, Japan and Italy currently see a decline of ten percent. [65]

During the 1990's, when the country ran a budget surplus, the economic expansion continued despite reduced household savings. Today when we run record fiscal deficits, a reduction in the personal savings rate makes the numbers more negative, thus raising alarms at both business and government levels. Are these personal savings really that significant? If so then how can the government encourage its people to save more? If not then why is aging such a major concern for the world?

The opinions on this are mixed, and here we present both sides. Economically, too much savings by households is just as bad for a nation as reduced savings. What matters is the overall macro-economic situation. Looking at the bigger picture, what matters more is the national savings rate. National savings are the net result of private savings (households and corporations) and public savings (government surpluses and deficits), and as long as there is enough savings to support the economic growth, it does not matter who is doing the saving. It is true that America is in debt; however, it is also true that increased savings are not necessarily an indication of economic growth. Germany is a perfect example. The country's personal savings rate was close to eleven percent in 2004; however, the economic expansion does not complement that. What is the solution then?

The government cannot do much to encourage savings besides changing the interest rates, but in a country like America where most savings are "paper" money (i.e., not backed by gold), that does very little good. In fact, it hinders corporate spending. So the change in savings patterns will demand a change of spending patterns at the consumer level. For consumers who are aging and retiring, where is the incentive to save?

Unless we have maintained a very health-conscious lifestyle during our youth and middle-aged years, beyond retirement the healthcare demands and expenditures rise considerably. For the US this means increased spending on healthcare benefits through Medicare. Unique to the US is also the problem of depleting Social Security funds. Medicare and Social Security are promises by the government to support its senior citizens after they retire. And to do so the employable workforce of the US contributes to the two funds during their working careers. So in essence, we pay up front for benefits later.

America will be hit by increased pressure on Social Security and Medicare funds as the baby boomer generation becomes eligible for it as early as 2008. The proportion of elderly people in America will increase significantly, and according to the Social Security Administration their numbers will double between 1995 and 2030. *"... Three years later, they will turn 65 and become eligible for Medicare. In the years that follow, the elderly population will steadily increase, putting serious strains on the budget because of increased expenditures for Social Security and for the Government's health programs serving this population."* [66]

SOCIAL SECURITY: A MERE PROMISE BY THE GOVERNMENT OR A RESPONSIBILITY?

Fundamentally, Social Security is a promise by the federal government to assist the retiring community in leading a comfortable and adequate lifestyle after they are no longer economically productive. It also allows retirees with dissimilar savings patterns to lead comparable lifestyles. However, this is about to change. According to the actuaries of the Social Security Administration, the ratio of working individuals to retirees will plummet to approximately 2:1 by 2030 compared against the current ratio of 3.3:1. [67] The excerpt below from the FY 2007 Budget Analytical Perspectives warns us about the gravity of the issue.

> *"Currently, the three major entitlement programs — Social Security, Medicare and Medicaid — account for 43 percent of non-interest Federal spending, up from*

thirty percent in 1980. By 2035, when the remaining baby boomers will be in their 70's and 80's, these three programs could easily account for nearly two-thirds of non-interest Federal spending. At the end of the projection period, in 2080, the figure rises to around three-quarters of non-interest spending. In other words, under an extension of current-law formulas, almost all of the budget, aside from interest, would go to these three programs alone. To say the least, that would severely reduce the flexibility of the budget, and the Government's ability to respond to new challenges."[68]

In addition to the above, President Bush said:

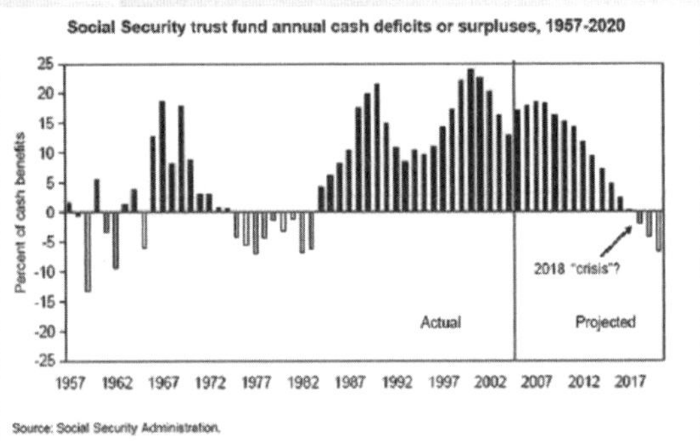

"Some in our country think that Social Security is a trust fund - in other words, there's a pile of money being accumulated. That's just simply not true. The money - payroll taxes going into the Social Security - are spent. They're spent on benefits and they're spent on government programs. There is no trust. We're on the ultimate pay-as-you-go system - what goes in comes out. ***And so, starting in 2018, what's going in - what's coming out is greater than what's going in. It says we've got a problem*** *[emphasis added]. And we'd better start dealing with it now. The longer we wait, the harder it is to fix the problem."* [69]

Though the graph clearly cites 2018 as the crisis point, what is more important is the year 2009. This is the year when the actual deficit in the Social Security funds starts. As the President stated, Social Security is a "pay as you go" system. The cash surpluses in the funds were transferred to the federal government in lieu of bonds. As the year 2012 approaches, the federal government will require additional savings to account for reductions in revenues of the Social Security fund. This is also correct, because the oldest of the baby boomers (1946-1964) will retire in 2011, which means 2012 will actually be the first year when they don't contribute but rather withdraw from the fund.

Given the shortage of Social Security funds, any additional debt accumulated between now and 2009 will only call for additional revenues in interest payments. In other words, if we continue to raise the debt we are only laying the foundation for not being able to keep our promise of Social Security to the seniors. It is estimated that in 2018 the Social Security deficit will require a transfer of $23 billion, or one tenth of GDP.[70] To add to the problem of Social Security, the government faces yet another challenge of the aging population: Medicare funding.

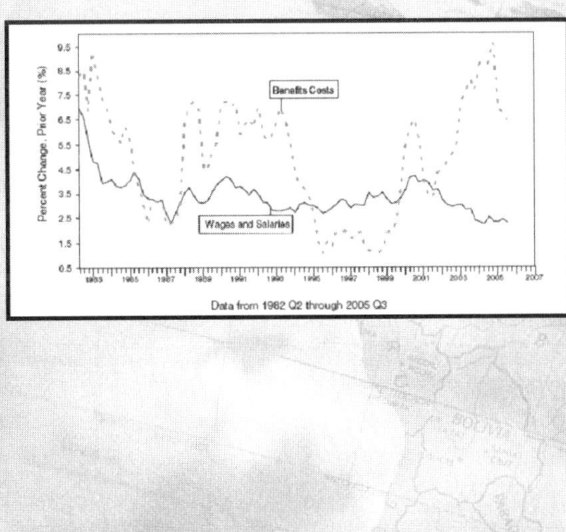

Healthcare System of the United States:

In addition to the above graph obtained from the Bureau of Labor Statistics, view these facts presented by the National Coalition on Health Care at http://www.nchc.org/facts/cost.shtml.

- Although nearly 46 million Americans are uninsured, the United States spends more on health care than other industrialized nations, and those countries provide health insurance to all their citizens.

- The annual premium that a health insurer charges an employer for a health plan covering a family of four averaged $10,800 in 2005. Workers contributed $2,713, or ten percent more than they did in 2004. The annual premiums for family coverage eclipsed the gross earnings for a full-time, minimum-wage worker ($10,712).

- A recent study by Harvard University researchers found that the average out-of-pocket medical debt for those who filed for bankruptcy was $12,000. The study noted that sixty-eight percent of those who filed for bankruptcy had health insurance. In addition, the study found that fifty percent of all bankruptcy filings were partly the result of medical expenses. Every thirty seconds in the United States, someone files for bankruptcy in the aftermath of a serious health problem.

- The percentage of Americans under age sixty-five whose family-level, out-of-pocket spending for health care, including health insurance, exceeds $2,000 a year rose from 37.3 percent in 1996 to 43.1 percent in 2003 - a 16 percent increase.

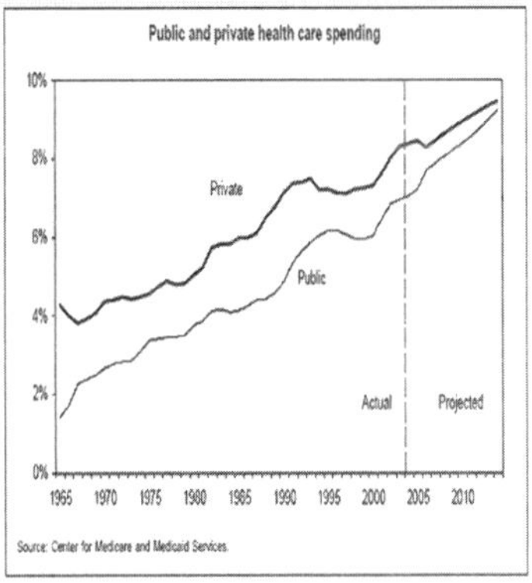

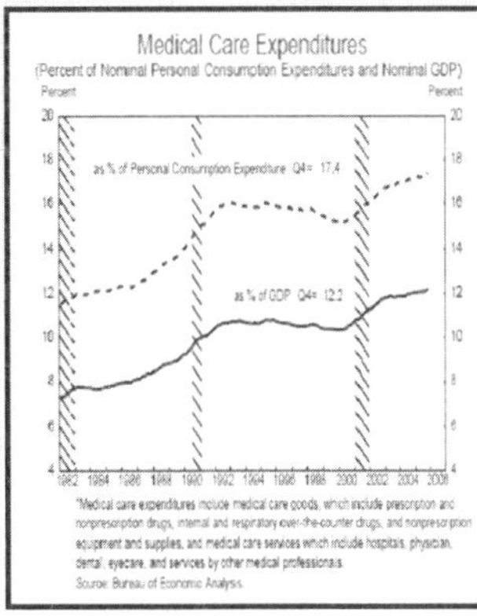

Additionally, the 2006 budget revealed Medicare spending will grow from 2.4% of GDP to 10.4% by 2075. It is no surprise that Medicare spending will outrun Social Security. This is partly due to the increasing number of baby boomers and the increased life spans due to advances in medical science. The question facing the government is how much per capita Medicare spending can it really afford? The majority of the increase in healthcare expenses is due to the new prescription drug benefit. Experts believe that the actual cost of the system will be much higher than the seventy-five-year estimated cost of $12.3 trillion, whereas Social Security's unfunded liability is $3.7 trillion.

The federal government is not the only one facing healthcare challenges; the increased costs are being felt by the private sector as well. Detailed overviews of the latest facts reveal a very disturbing picture. If, for the sake of argument, we assume that the government will achieve the promised fifty-percent reduction in budget deficit and continue its fiscal discipline, will the people of America be able to bear the increasing costs of quality healthcare? Probably not.

Individuals today spend close to eighteen percent of their personal expenses on medical costs. In addition to the fact that almost eighteen percent of personal expenses is devoted to medical expenses, it is interesting to note that the increase of healthcare as a percentage of GDP and the increase in personal consumption are closely following each other. This is interesting not because the percentage is increasing but more because when we see the numbers of GDP increase we rarely consider it from the proper perspective. If there was an increase in GDP, what component caused that increase? In most cases it is the consumption increase; however, if healthcare costs caused the increase then in addition to generating more jobs there is also a flip side to it: the increased costs.

True to its complexity, the New Economy creates new challenges for the healthcare industry, also. Additionally, obesity in the US is rising, raising further issues for the already over-burdened healthcare system. Obesity, in all likelihood, is the next worst healthcare nightmare for the US unless we change our eating and moving habits. According to the American Demographics analysis, one third of the global population aged fifteen and older is either overweight or obese. The United States of America is the "supreme" world leader in this, too. The United States accounts for twenty-three percent of the world's obese population.

Whether due to aging or obesity, healthcare costs are on the rise and will continue be do so. Why are the medical treatments so expensive? Is it simply because the doctors charge more? Or is it because the free market principles of "competitiveness" have not influenced the medical profession yet?

Having said this, from a regulatory perspective, while treating the health care market as a free market is a good idea, one need remember the consumer segments; we are dealing with humans here and not commodities. There will always be a strong personal element to this field; the principles of free market may not be directly applicable. For instance, the patient age varies from newborn children to elderly seniors. The current population of the US is leaning more towards the older end of the continuum as the baby boomer generation increases while the birth rate decreases. What happens if it gets converted to a true free market in which consumers (patients) can shop around globally and make a buying decision? Clearly, the young to middle-aged or late middle-aged group benefits, and the seniors, who are well into retirement and not physically or educationally equipped to search the globe, are at a disadvantage. [71] This brings us back to the eternal question: so what should be done? What is the solution to the ever-increasing healthcare costs, and how does the common man meet them?

The government today is struggling to find an answer that pleases everyone. And somewhere within this dilemma probably lies the solution, also. Maybe there is no single solution to this problem. Maybe the states need to look at their individual demographics and develop plans that are unique to the changing demands of their regional populations. The federal government guidelines will ensure fundamental health care coverage while the state guidelines will cover situations unique to them. For instance, states with a higher population of retirees compared to those who have a higher percentage of homeless or higher percentage of middle-aged working professionals would obviously need different healthcare plans.

The Wall Street Journal article "Healthcare for Everyone, We Found a Way" provides an in-depth look into the possible reforms. Fundamentally, the article discusses the inherent human nature of exploiting the system when possible. There will always be people who will not buy health insurance nor pay for it unless there is an emergency. Emergency care, by law, cannot be denied. So, such individuals can get away by getting subsidized emergency care; but somebody has to pay, and it is either the insured population directly through higher premiums or everyone in society indirectly through higher taxes. This article also affirms our earlier theory that plans have to be customized to each state. A generic plan that works for all will not be possible if the demographics of the country continue to change dramatically.

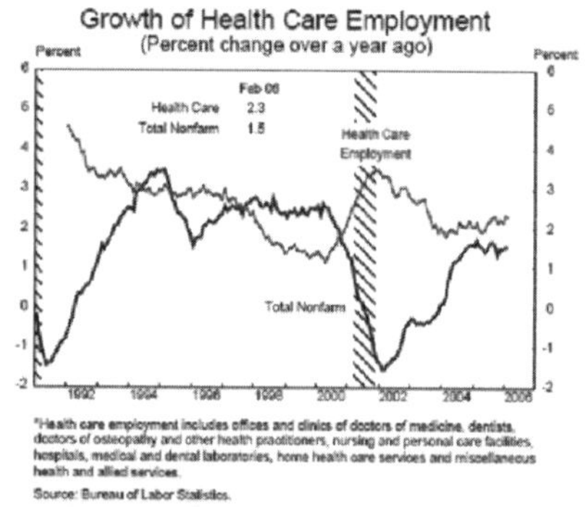

*Health care employment includes offices and clinics of doctors of medicine, dentists, doctors of osteopathy and other health practitioners, nursing and personal care facilities, hospitals, medical and dental laboratories, home health care services and miscellaneous health and allied services.

Source: Bureau of Labor Statistics.

While state reforms are making efforts to provide health insurance to all, the policy makers need to remember that it needs to be *affordable*. It would be inappropriate to make any dollar estimates here without actually conducting research on the costs and prices; however, it would be safe to say that most families may not be comfortable spending more than two hundred dollars a month, in 2005 dollars, on insurance. Policies for healthcare will have to account for the additional increase in energy and gas prices, since those are necessities, whereas visits to the doctor's office will be on a contingency basis. Hence, affordability is of prime importance.

Dipping into savings or increased income often accommodates increased costs of healthcare. It has been clearly demonstrated many times that the increase in income or salaries is minimal due to increases in the global labor supply, so that leaves us with savings. Sadly, we know now that America's savings rate is at the lowest ever.

By now you should be able to see the connection between seemingly disconnected dots. The America that was once called the land of opportunity, where no dream was too big to realize, is now called the nation of debt. However, we still have many other dots to connect before we see what the face of our nation will really look like.

CHAPTER 10

THE FACE OF AMERICA IS CHANGING: MINORITIES! WHO ARE THEY?

The face of America continues to change. In the twentieth century, Americans were classified as two extreme spectrums of the color band: white or black. Now America is seeing the middle color: brown. It is true; America is browning. According to the census bureau, by 2050 fifty-percent of the US population will be a combination of the current minority races, with Hispanics and Asians being the two dominant ethnic groups. [72]

Minority: this word once represented anyone who was not Caucasian. However, it is now time that we change the definition of this word. The trend is reversing. Racial majorities will soon be minorities. The twenty-first century demands not only changing the very definition of the term "minority," but it is quite possible that the word will be eliminated from many media and government publications. Why? Because being a minority means something only when there is "actually" a majority to compare it against.

You might not agree with this today, but the reality is that the world is once again merging, as many believe it was intended to. Just as goods flow freely across nations, soon individuals will, too, for the laws of free trade also apply to people. The recent debate on immigration has allowed for debate and discussion across both print and broadcast media. On January 7, 2004, President Bush put forward his proposal for a "guest worker" plan for illegal immigrants, or the "undocumented workers" of this country. It has been two years now, and the debate continues.

One of the most common arguments against immigration is that these immigrants will take away American jobs and hurt American wages. Is this really true? There have been multiple studies designed to find an answer, but the results are not as conclusive as we expected. [73]

Economically speaking, and assuming all else constant, an influx of cheap labor will bring wages down; but this is going to depend on regional demographics. The population of immigrant workers is very high in Los Angeles compared to Indianapolis or some other conservative mid-west areas. So while the influx of immigration or cheap labor is high in LA, it is not so high in many other areas. Hence, the influence on wages in LA will obviously be higher than in states such as Indiana.

Take a look at the professional world. While illegal immigration is not a problem here, there are many jobs that are offered to H1-B immigrants, typically at reduced or lower wages then an equivalent US citizen would require. The major corporations have succeeded in convincing Congress that there is a "shortage" of certain professionals, especially in the field of information and technology; therefore, the US needs to allow more foreign IT workers to be hired. In fact there are no shortages; it is just another example of the greed found in big business and major corporations. These are prime conditions that would allow them to pay less in wages and not provide any benefits. As the debate on immigration continues, businesses need to think ahead. If the eleven million or so illegal immigrants do receive citizenship status, for a business owner or manager it means an influx of legal labor at reduced wages and increased administrative costs.

First and foremost the increase in labor will mostly be hourly labor, and many may not speak English. In order for them to receive respectable employment, both businesses and government will either have to make extra effort to make their documents available in different languages or educate the immigrant work force and assist them in settling here. In addition to handling the language challenge, the PR policies of most companies will have to adapt and be more sensitive toward different cultures. This means not only respecting and recognizing the differences but also changing policies to reflect them. For instance, we may see a major change in what holidays we recognized and grant for people of different nationalities.

Businesses today fear that as the issue gains prominence, and because the federal government is already struggling with increased costs of war and reduced resources for other activities, they might have to share this burden. For businesses this means increased legal and administrative responsibilities. Additionally, under the current proposal there is a strong penalty for hiring illegal workers. So that's a double dip for the business owners. First, they have to verify the nationality of their employees, and if they falter they will be penalized with fines. *The House of Representatives' immigration bill will require all employers to use the Social Security system to verify authenticity and working status eligibility. The penalty for non-compliance ranges from $10,000 to $40,000 with a possible 30-year sentence for repeat offenders.* [74] While most businesses agree that to curb illegal immigration they will have to play their role, they also don't want to be fined if the verification system is not very reliable or updated regularly.

In addition to the burden of sharing the legal responsibilities, many small businesses such as agriculture, gardening, janitorial, moving companies and restaurants have often relied on the immigrant population to fill the gaps between the demand and supply for these types of jobs. These and many other businesses have relied on the guest-worker program to fill the gap. According to the Pew Hispanic Center there are close to eleven million illegal or undocumented workers in the United States, and the idea that America can function efficiently without them is just misguided. Opponents of the guest worker program argue that it exploits the immigrant population because these workers will often accept pay lower than the minimum wage.

The legal employment of immigrant workers is also facing a new trend, especially in the lower wage market: union centers. Janice Fine, an assistant professor of labor studies and employment at Rutgers University, says that in 1992 there were fewer than five centers nationwide, while today there are about 140 centers in eighty US cities and rural areas across the nation. [75] While these union centers can assist the immigrant population to settle faster in their new roles, they can also mean additional costs for companies and the US Government, which translates into additional taxes.

With blue or white collar workers the key to retaining employees in the New Economy will not be so much about increased salaries but more about making them feel good about the places they work. Recognizing and respecting the growing emotional needs of workers to feel welcome at their workplaces is the prime challenge facing employers, both big and small. Even more, as with the continued war and anti-foreigner sentiments, more Americans are turning into isolationists. While isolationism is not yet a publicly debated subject, it has very strong undercurrents that are beginning to surface as strong waves both in the political and business worlds.

According to a recent Pew poll, forty-two percent of Americans agree that America should mind its own business. They don't want to deal with a global world. [76]

GLOBALIZATION: A FRIEND OR FOE?

Globalization is a term we hear a lot today. What is globalization? The most common perception of globalization is the integration of economic platforms across geographical boundaries. And that is probably where the problem is, too. Globalization does not only imply assimilating economic goals but also merging the social and cultural boundaries. Cultural globalization for the US is often considered the "Mexicanization" of America. The Bush administration's effort supporting immigration is often criticized on the grounds that the assimilation will be so complete that no culture will have an individual identity. While this may be true, it is also true that if the immigration numbers are large the need and the will to assimilate will be small and may disappear completely.

For America the problem is even more distinctive because the majority of the cultural change is coming from Mexico and not Spanish speakers. We emphasize this point because often in America anyone who speaks Spanish is considered to be Mexican. And with the current debate on immigration, this assumption lends to a negative connotation. The question from a business perspective is not so much whether the employable base is from Mexico or Puerto-Rico but whether the globalization of cultures is really possible.

An article in *The Washington Post*, "Together in Bicultural Business," illustrates this point beautifully. The article suggests that businesses dealing with a bicultural environment need to remember that their strategies will be governed more by language, cultural, and multi-ethnic issues than by geographical boundaries. Understanding this point is also important because as the baby boomers retire many of the younger workers will be immigrants, and they become the target consumer base for many industries.

The globalization of culture is important, but the two critical questions facing the world are "How fast?" and "To what extent?" Americans have and will continue to blame the after-effects of globalization, reduced wages, and increasing unemployment on immigrants. Their fears are not unfounded, though. "Globalization and Job Loss – from Manufacturing to Services" by Lori G. Kletzer identifies the "off–shoring" shift from manufacturing to services. [77] Additionally, Deloitte and Touché estimate that by 2008 the majority of the world finance companies will have relocated nearly

two million jobs to low-cost countries. In 2003 Bardhan and Kroll estimated that **fourteen million workers** were vulnerable to job loss from outsourcing. The author further cites preliminary estimates for risk of job loss in the service sector averaging approximately two percent to three percent, compared to seven percent for manufacturing. While the estimate is small and very preliminary, upward movement in job relocation for the service sector, mainly in the finance, insurance, and professional business services, has begun. Another study released within the same volume ***"What Do We Know About Job Loss in the United States? Evidence from the Displaced Workers Survey, 1984–2004"*** uses the 2004 Displaced Worker Survey to understand the effect of globalization and job loss.

It is interesting to note that while the economic output and growth of the country increased after 2001, the rates of job loss and unemployment also increased. Additionally, the new knowledge economy jobs that were supposed to be created due to a US shift from a manufacturing base to a service base have **not** occurred. The reality is that job growth in the US has not kept up with the increased population growth. [78]

A recent report by Goldman Sachs collectively dubs these emerging economies as BRICs (Brazil, Russia, India and China). In addition to highlighting the growing influence of BRICs on the global economy, the report presents this interesting fact: collectively these countries contributed nearly as much as the United States to the world economy. While the US continues to dominate, the increasing economic power of other nations takes us back to an earlier question. Why is it that the slowdown in the US economy has not influenced the global economy as much as it did earlier? The answer lies in the fact that the rising economic power of other countries means that the world can now survive without being dependent on the US economy. Additionally, when the US economy slows, the developing world can provide the resources for our economy to continue. This is exactly why the US has not felt a downturn in the economy despite increasing energy costs and the destruction of New Orleans and its associated petroleum refining capacity by hurricane Katrina. This illustrates the power of the New Economy: no nation dominates. In a recent independent survey it was found that US economic competitiveness had fallen significantly over the past year, as high budget/trade deficits and corruption have damaged America's business environment. This has resulted in the US being ranked 6th in global competitiveness from the top spot a year ago. The nations of Switzerland, Finland, Sweden, Denmark and Singapore were the respective winners. The influence of the US economy will continue to decline, and we will continue to experience a reduction in our overall living standards when compared to other countries, unless we implement massive changes in both our foreign policies and our domestic agenda.

The Old Economy way was simply to "follow the US." The New Economy way strives to learn from the past and improve upon it, thus giving the developing nations a tremendous advantage. If the problems of decreased savings and increased job loss were not enough, America's population is facing the additional cost of misguided energy and education policies. The cost of everyday living in America is increasing.

INCREASED COSTS OF AMERICAN LIVING:

In his 2006 State-of-the-Union address, President Bush made a very honest confession: "America is addicted to oil." The speech also proposed replacing seventy-five percent of the oil imports from Middle East by the year 2025, a noble thought indeed. If the Middle East does receive such an oil shock, what will happen? The price of oil will skyrocket. Additionally, while President Bush correctly identifies clean coal technologies as the gateway to reducing

America's addiction to oil, the policies just don't promise the same. So far the administration has literally given away millions in federal grants toward clean technologies with little result. Clearly, additional funding is not the key to promoting these technologies. What is needed is restricting the use of coal-based fuel. The policies proposed are not encouraging fuel economy in vehicles, they are not penalizing the continued production of gas-guzzlers, and more importantly these policies are doing nothing to prevent Americans from consuming more oil. Until that shift happens, America's addiction to oil will continue, even if it is at the expense of reduced savings and a depleted environment.

The energy crisis is not limited to national borders. If the developed nations of the world do not reduce their dependence, the oil producing nations will have an upper hand in many political situations. Take Russia as an example. Russian president Vladimir Putin asked the Ukraine to pay the market value of gas rather than the subsidized rate it was paying for purely political reasons. The intervention of the international community prevented this from happening, but the world should learn from this lesson. The oil-producing nations are at war with the oil-consuming ones.

Global warming is a challenge faced not only by the US but also by developing nations. Recent reports have suggested numbers of automobiles as high as one billion by 2020 globally. This is not because of a sudden increase in the US market but more because of increases in demand for cars in China and India and other parts of the developing world. Automobiles are one of the largest sources of environmental pollution. Despite stringent emission standards, pollution continues to increase because of a mixed fleet of vehicles in the developing parts of the world. For instance, in the Asian region it is not unusual to see motorbikes, public buses, cars, and bicycles driving on the same road.

Additionally, due to increased gasoline prices diesel-powered vehicles are very popular there. Unlike the US where cars are a necessity, they are a luxury there, and having one symbolizes superior social status. So as the disposable income increases in these regions, the appetite for cars also increases. While this may be good news for a struggling automotive industry, it is not necessarily good news for our planet.

In addition to polluting the environment they also increase the demand for gasoline. With prices potentially reaching as high as $70 a barrel in the future and the political instability increasing in the oil-producing regions, the likelihood of prices increasing further is even higher. It is an undeniable fact that the demand for cars is not going to reduce either within or outside the US. But what can be done to save the future generations and ourselves is to change our perception of how much of a car we really do need. The US society is different from the other emerging economies in many other ways than simply consumption and lifestyle. Developing nations, just by the nature of things there, have become used to many situations that are considered unacceptable within the US.

Earlier we discussed the differences between the education patterns of the two countries and how those differences translated to varied professional skills. Unfortunately, while the US education system does encourage self-expression and freedom to choose, it does not emphasize enough the core fundamentals of learning. Often, with the advanced tools available, the core tasks were considered a waste of time, and students have been allowed to replace mental calculation with electronic devices. The task of actually writing reports has been replaced with keyboards and software. The result is that we need MS Word to check our spelling and grammar and calculators to perform basic addition and subtraction.

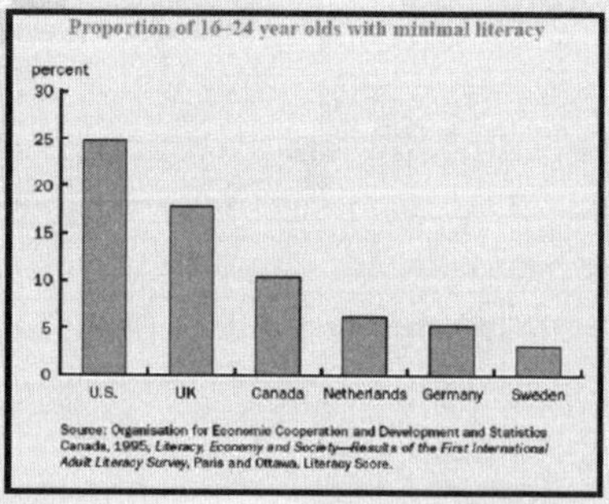

However, now that we have realized and recognized the importance of education it is important to reemphasize the importance of these core fundamentals among students, teachers, and parents alike. The emphasis on strong fundamentals needs to extend beyond the school boundaries to homes. Parents can play a key role in better preparing their kids for the New Economy. Unfortunately, parents are strapped for time; and with debt levels rising, not many have the option of being single income families. So the time constraint comes into play. Where and how do we spend more time with family? The answer probably lies in understanding the fact that activities expand with time and space. So, as such, there will never be extra time; the key is to find different ways to use it.

The US leads the world in minimal literacy also. The world's supreme power has the largest number of illiterates. It's harsh, but it's true. When you take this into account it is not surprising that off-shoring has increased. The supply of specialized and skilled workers is just not enough to meet the demand of an increasingly technology-based service industry or to satisfy the increasing employment opportunities in alternative energy technologies. [79]

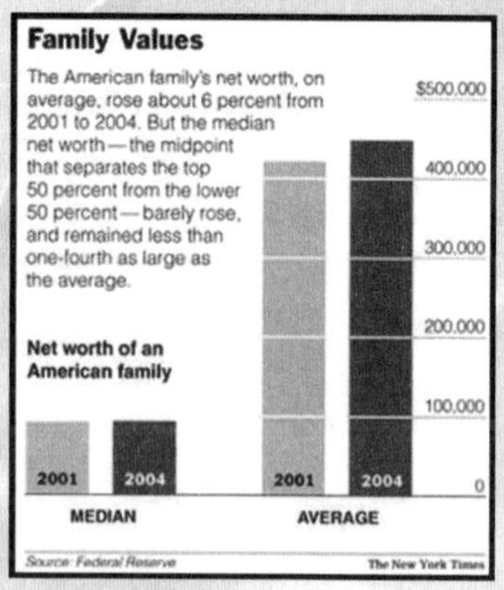

Take into account the fact that the disposable income for the middle class families has been on the decline. Daniel Gross, in his article "When Sweet Statistics Clash with a Sour Mood," discusses the idea of measuring true income growth by measuring the median income. The median income is essentially the mid point between the top fifty percent and the lower fifty percent, the line that divides the haves from the have-nots. When one looks at those numbers the median income has gone nowhere. [80]

To that, when one adds the additional cost of gas, increased housing prices, the increased cost of education, and the continued high costs of the the wars we are fighting, one can understand why the American middle class does not relate to the government's claim of having a robust economy.

BUSINESSES: BE READY FOR CHANGE

America cannot continue to play an important role in the coming years unless there is a radical shift in the US's complacent and arrogant approach. So far the current administration has operated somewhere between sound economic theories and Utopia, and what it lacks are real life solutions, solutions that actually work.

The increased trend of off-shoring is a case in point. Free trade, as any economist will tell you, works and creates a win-win situation for all. But this has not been the case for the United States. Why? The Old Economy principles are being applied to New Economy issues. For instance, the free trade of goods applies to goods that are actually boxed and shipped, not to goods that are shipped over the Internet from one country to another. Yes, there are still goods being shipped, but look at the supplier base available to a single customer. He or she can buy from anywhere in the world. Similarly, suppliers are competing for buyers across the globe. While specialization works, in an Internet economy the magnitude of available options is drastically different when compared to a pen and paper economy.

What does this mean for you as an entrepreneur or business manager? It clearly implies significantly increased focus on the customer. Additionally, entrepreneurship focused on personal services, such as real estate, will be more successful than impersonal services. For example, if your realtor is in California and your house is in Florida, the Internet does you little good. But if you need your taxes prepared then distance does not matter, as long as they are filed according to US laws, and with the new e-file option, available tax preparation professionals can be anywhere in the world.

The most pressing issue for many business leaders currently is how to revive the large scale-manufacturing sector of the US. Will the small-to-medium-size manufacturing companies continue to succeed? The prudent choice would be to focus efforts on these; there is a strong possibility that the government might just have to assist in this matter with some form of incentives.

In economics the concept of specialization and trade benefits emphasizes that specialization allows countries to produce what they are best at and trade for the others. This way, trading partners can exchange for goods and produce their specialty at lower cost. When we extend this concept it is intuitive that, in addition to specializing in a particular product, nations may specialize in a particular phase of the product manufacturing cycle. The US has always been a leader in innovation. While visionaries such as Henry Ford introduced mass manufacturing, lower cost nations have been able to apply the principles at even lower prices. Understanding this is key to the success of the US as a leader in the business world. The amount of reinvestment required to revive manufacturing is going to be considerably higher than continuing and encouraging innovation.

Having said this, it is important to recognize the fact that manufacturing is not limited to automotive or electronics; there are many other manufacturing facilities that are connected to industries that will probably not be outsourced, at least in the near future. Take, for instance, the construction industry. It includes everything from infrastructure development to residential buildings. The US style of construction is pre-cut and pre-cast. The DIY attitude of the country will always create demand for products. And within construction there are many parts mass manufactured by small-to–medium-sized companies. This is another avenue where the US can create jobs and increase exports.

As the disposable income in developing nations increases, the demand for upscale hardware and related construction items will increase, too. In the recent report "The Future Success of Small and Medium Manufacturers, Challenges and Policy Issues" by R.S.M. McGladrey, the report clearly identifies the success of manufacturing to be within the small-to-medium-sized manufacturers (also referred as SMM). According to the National Association of Manufacturers (NAM), small companies have 500 or fewer employees, whereas medium sized manufacturers are those who have 500-2,500 employees. The report brings out many interesting statistics. A few of the more important ones are:

- SMMs account for forty percent of the US production.
- SMMs account for eight million employees within manufacturing.
- SMMs are responsible for fifteen percent of US exports.

Just these three simple facts state the potential of harboring and investing in the small-to-medium business sector. SMMs are also characterized by a unique customer relationship. Because their businesses are small enough to still be personalized, they listen to their customers first and then develop the products. Many times their products and solutions are customized to their clients. Such a unique partnership ensures customer loyalty and also stimulates collaborative innovation. Innovation for products that are actually required by customers secures future revenue potential.

Internal controls are another challenge faced by SMMs, and they are handled quite differently from the large conglomerates. Huge corporations are often under pressure to meet stock market expectations; thus, decisions are often short term. On the contrary, SMMs are often family-run businesses, the stock market pressures are absent, and the management can focus on long-term consequences and growth. This is especially challenging because their resources, both financial and intellectual, are limited. The report identifies many challenges faced by the SMMs; in an effort to stay focused, we concentrate on innovation and retaining our innovative edge in the world.

Every country, industry, business, and product goes through respective life cycles. The key to retaining our innovative edge is better education so that qualified employees can replace the talented retiring community. Intellectual innovation has been and will always be the strength of this country. Cultural and educational differences, discussed earlier, once again play an important role. Remember, the American education system allows students to choose easier subjects and gain credits. While this approach keeps them from mastering mathematics or science, it encourages overall development and growth. It allows them to mix and match sciences, and very often that is the key to innovation: the ability to look at things differently.

The country as a whole will be better off investing in improved education for its citizens rather than trying to revive the manufacturing sector. This is because the question is not simply one of reviving it, it is a question of extent and cost. The automotive industry is dominated by Toyota and Honda, and now the Chinese company Cherry is planning to introduce its car in the US as early as 2007. [81]

It would be more sensible for the US to invest in developing, creating and harboring knowledge-oriented jobs with the appropriate supporting education and training being provided.

WILL WE RETAIN OUR SUPREMACY?

Unlike prior eras when we were the supreme economic power, in the new era we will have company, and in some cases, lots of company. That is, in many ways, frightening for the individual in terms of how to survive in this new world, this New Economy.

Nations in the twenty-first century will specialize in certain industries. With globalization and reductions in trade barriers, it is unlikely that one nation will dominate the world economy. Change happens. It's a reality whether we are receptive to it or not, and the best part is, very often we don't even realize that it's happening. This is exactly what happened during the shift along the continuum of Old Economy to New Economy. The Old Economy involved working for a single company over a lifetime, whereas the New Economy encourages flexibility and entrepreneurship. The Old Economy laws favored monopolies, and today the law favors free trade. Earlier we talked about preventing layoffs. Today we talk about upgrading the skill set and improving the education system. And last but not least, the Old Economy blamed companies for not issuing product warnings for the obvious, and today we talk about innovation and how to protect it. Remember, *"One who thinks he knows all, has a lot to learn."* [82]

Understanding the depth and simplicity of the above sentence will allow you to look beyond America. As a society we will thus learn to respect different cultures and perspectives and hopefully regain respect globally. The onus of looking beyond the obvious will be on the individual. It is the individual who will have to adapt, learn new skills, assimilate into a multi-cultural environment, and widen his/her outlook. The answer, while complex, can be achieved by anyone with the ideas and energy to create. To quote Eric Hoffer: "In times of Change, the learners inherit the Earth, while the learned find themselves beautifully equipped to deal with a world that no longer exists."

CHAPTER 11

Food for Thought: Join the Dots

"A friendly eye could never see such faults."

– William Shakespeare,
Julius Caesar

CHAPTER 11

Here is some further food for thought. Hopefully these items will make you think…and act! Connect the dots and draw your own conclusions. We believe that the writing is on the wall, and the time to act is now! The issues are in alphabetical order, so you can find your own favorite! Many of the statements appearing below are taken from newspapers, articles and reports.

CURRENCY - THE DOLLAR

The dollar is falling and doing so at a quickening pace. It's falling against the Euro, the Japanese yen, the Swiss Franc, the British pound, and even the Brazilian real. In this new phase of the economy, not only will dollars buy you less but there could also be fewer dollars available as foreign investors cut off the flow of dollars from Asia, Europe and the Middle East. This could have a number of effects, including the following:

- Higher interest rates on long-term bonds, commercial loans, and all forms of mortgages.
- Crack open the US housing market.
- Force the Fed to start a whole new round of interest rate hikes.
- Send contra-dollar investments (gold, silver, oil and other commodities) surging.

Alan Greenspan, former Federal Reserve Chairman, warned that the dollar was being challenged as the world's resource currency. "We're beginning to see some move from the dollar to the Euro," he stated. His comments led to a decline in the value of the dollar. This comment was made at the Commercial Financial Association. [83]

ECONOMY-BUDGET DEFICIT

The US Government's current account deficit widened in the first quarter to a record $195.1 billion. This represents 6.4% of the total gross domestic economy. The US budget deficit reached a record $413 billion, requiring foreigners to pump money into the economy at an unprecedented rate.

We are experiencing the fastest rise in federal spending since FDR by spending 20.8 cents of every dollar the economy generates.

The House was scheduled to pass a $2.8 trillion budget for 2007, which projects an additional $3 trillion of debt in the next five years, mainly due to the biggest military buildup in decades, in contrast to a $236 billion budget surplus in 2000 under President Clinton.

EDUCATION

India graduated almost a million more students than the US. China graduates twice as many students with degrees as the US and has six times as many graduate students majoring in engineering. Today most, if not all, jobs allowing you to support a family require a post-secondary education.

EXECUTIVE PAY

Departing executives Philip Purcell of Morgan Stanley received $113 million, Harry Stonecypher of Boeing received $600,000/year, Carly Fiorina of Hewlett-Packard received $21 million, Franklyn Raines at Fanny Mae received $1.4 million/year, and Scott Livengood of Krispy Kreme received $46,000/month." [84]

In America the ratio of pay received by a CEO and a worker in 2004 was 301 to 1. In Japan it was 10 to 1.

Eighteen percent of all working Americans did not earn enough to keep a family of four above the official poverty line, even when working forty hours per week for fifty weeks of the year. The average wage was $12,195 in 1990.

Pfizer's former chief executive Henry McKinnell, who was forced into an early retirement, will get a package worth more than $180 million including an estimated $82.3 million in pension benefits, $77.9 million in deferred compensation, and $20.7 million in cash and stock. He also will receive an annual pension of $6.6 million.

GOVERNMENT

It's not OK to lie us into war.

It's not OK to stop investigations into the truth by saying that it's secret information.

It's not OK to out CIA agents for political reasons.

The Bush administration has spent nearly $43 billion dollars over the last five years on missile defense systems, with little confidence in their capability to protect the United States.

Citizens Against Waste reported that $29 Billion had been set aside by members of Congress chiefly in the annual appropriations bills to benefit lobbyists and large corporations.

HEALTHCARE COSTS

Recent studies show that the US does a poorer job than any other industrialized country at proving primary medical care to its citizens, particularly to those with less education and income. [85]

Health care costs are up fifty percent since 2000. Forty-five million people are going without healthcare, including 6.6 million in California. [86]

Americans are more likely to have diabetes (forty-two percent), high blood pressure (thirty-two percent), and arthritis (twelve percent) than Canadians or citizens of other countries. The existence of a National Health Program is believed to account for at least part of this difference.

Medicare's funding shortfall over the next seventy-five years will reach $32.4 trillion, or nearly three times the current size of the entire US economy. Of this, about a third will result from the President's unfunded prescription drug benefit.

HOUSING

Almost a third of US home buyers were forced into risky, interest-only mortgages in 2005 as a record jump in house prices drove affordability to a twenty-year high, according to a Harvard University study recently released. The average mortgage payments in 2005 rose to twenty-four percent of the median income, the highest since 1984. [87]

The biggest single driver of global growth in the last five years has been the propensity for US households to go deeper into debt. For example, twenty-nine percent of borrowers who took out mortgages in the US last year have no equity in their homes or owe more than their houses are worth.

IMAGE ABROAD - US

"It is problematic to welcome as a guest a politician who wages unconstitutional wars, uses falsified secret reports as an excuse to do so, is willing to preemptively deploy nuclear weapons, who tolerates kidnappings, torture, and illegal detention camps as a means of security policy," said an Austrian Government Official on the visit by President Bush to Europe. This speaks to a sharp decline in America's prestige in the world.

INCOMES

Average incomes and net worth growth was the weakest in ten years.

The average profit-per-partner at the nation's largest law firms passed the $1 million mark with the top ten firms booking profit-per-partner of $2 million.

INFLATION

Gas prices are up sixty percent. High energy prices have sapped consumer and business spending and depressed economic growth by as much as one percent since late 2003. Given the impact of basic materials on inflation, it is noteworthy to see the oil company profits picture:

"Occidental Petroleum: forty-five percent higher earnings, Valero: fifty-nine percent higher earnings." [88]

In the last three years, oil prices have nearly tripled and gasoline costs have nearly doubled.

INTERNET

Total number of web sites in 1995 was 1.3 million; in December of 2004 it was 8 billion!

There are 200 million searches each day on Google.

JOBS

Silicon Valley technology companies pushed Congress into doubling the number of H-1B worker visas to 115,000 for foreign workers in the science, math, technology and engineering areas.

Since 2002, Hewlett Packard has laid off thirty percent of its employees worldwide to cut costs and improve operations, while funneling back office employment to lower-paid employees in Asia, Eastern Europe, and Latin America.

IBM Corp plans to triple its investment in India to $6 billion over the next three years and has increased staff locally to 43,000.

Microsoft Corp. said it doubled its workforce in India with an investment of $1.7 billion in four years.

Intel Corp announced a $1 billion India investment plan.

Cisco Systems Inc. plans to invest $1.1 billion in India over the next three years.

President Bush announced his economic plan is working, with unemployment improved to five percent with the latest monthly figures.

30,000 jobs are to be cut by GM by 2008.

2.7M jobs were lost from early 2001 through August 2003.

Ford Motor Co. Chief Executive Alan Mulally said that the auto maker is moving faster than expected to shrink US capacity to better match market demand. Ford is shaving more than 30,000 U.S. hourly jobs this year and closing seven assembly plants by 2010.

H-P & Kodak both announced restructuring plans to cut costs. H-P will lose around ten percent of its staff or 14,500 jobs over the next eighteen months and freeze pension and medical benefits. Kodak, which gave notice of 15,000 job losses at the start of 2004, said it would cut an additional 10,000 jobs to help quicken its move into digital products.

Two American carmakers reported poor second-quarter results. General Motors reported a net loss of $286M versus a profit in the same period of $1.4B. Ford's net profit fell by nineteen percent to $946M with its North American car business recoding a pre-tax loss of $1B.

Merck to slash 7,000 jobs, or eleven percent of its workforce, with sixty percent of the reductions in manufacturing. The company also plans to close five plants.

In Atlanta, two major automotive plants will close by 2008 at a cost of 5,000 jobs. Delta Airlines filed for bankruptcy and is expected to eliminate 10,000 jobs by mid 2007. BellSouth laid off 1,500 employees, and after the merger with AT&T, a further 10,000 jobs will be cut. Two military bases are closing eliminating 5,000 jobs.

Heinz to cut 2,700 jobs, fifteen plants to cut costs and boost profits.

Lego to cut 1,200 jobs in the US and shift the production to Mexico where the costs are cheaper.

It is estimated that thirty percent of high tech jobs will be shifted off-shore by 2015.

Median pay among chief executives running most of the nation's 100 largest companies soared twenty-five percent to $17.9M, in comparison with the 3.1% average gain by typical American workers. This excludes other perks such as bonus, travel, options, club memberships, stock etc. It also excludes the golden pensions they receive that range from $2M to $6.5M a year. In the case of Cendant, the CEO took over $133M in pay, yet the company lost twenty-one percent of its value. Similarly, Hank McKinnel, the CEO of Pfizer, has had a paycheck of some $65M in compensation and will receive an $83M pension when he retires; however, during his tenure Pfizer's shares lost forty-six percent of their value.

Sixteen percent of employees had their pay frozen in 2000.

Of the recently announced small improvement in the overall employment figures in the nation, 50,000 went into retail, 30,000 into hotels and restaurants, and 29,000 into healthcare; however, all of these represent the lowest paying jobs. It is noteworthy that 4,000 manufacturing jobs were lost in the same period, and seventy-nine percent of people now work in the service sector; and with corporate downsizing, this will expand.

LOBBYING

Wealthy people should not have influence over senior government officials because of their wealth. They should not impose their demands on the needs of poor people. ~ Iranian President Mahmoud Ahmadinejad.

In 2005, Americans spent $134 billion on fast food, more than on college education, personal computers or even new cars. The fast food industry aggressively targets poor people with food that is cheap because of government subsidies for the meatpacking industry, corn, and other crops and federal government loans for fast food franchises.

MEDIA

CBS Evening News devoted one minute and thirty nine seconds to coverage of Iraq on a day when Iraq was close to civil war with at least seventy-six Iraqis killed and 179 wounded in sectarian attacks. They devoted the same amount of time to Anna Nicole Smith's appearance in front of the Supreme Court.

MINORITIES FINANCIAL OUTLOOK

Until recently African Americans have had just fifty-six percent of the economic status of whites in spite of a rebounding economy. The median net worth for African American families is less than 1/10th of the median for white families. Similarly, unemployment for black people is ten percent, compared with 4.4% for whites.

NAFTA

After the demise of the coal industry and the textile industry due to free trade agreements such as NAFTA, jobs have gone to Honduras and China, as this has encouraged companies to lay off American workers to produce goods more cheaply abroad and then import the goods back into the US. This shows how the global economy contributes to the growing inequality in America, with the gap between the rich and the poor doubling in the last three decades until it is now wider than in the days of the Great Depression.

OIL

Exxon banked $10.5B in third quarter profit. That was the second highest quarterly profit ever posted by a publicly traded company. Revenue was $99.6B. The government has made more money on gas sales than all the big oil companies combined. Since 1977, governments have collected $1.34 trillion in tax revenues, or an average of 45.9 cents per gallon. [89]

POVERTY

37 million Americans are living in poverty.

TAXES

The current Bush Administration has followed a Free Spending Policy with tax breaks of $2 trillion, mainly for the wealthy; however, at the same time it allowed a record national debt of over $8.3 trillion with a request this be raised to $10 trillion in anticipation of spending even more!

The Senate has just voted to extend the $70 billion dollars in tax cuts, even though we are running a $300 billion deficit.

In 2004, ninety-four percent of major corporations paid less than five percent of their income in taxes. The actual corporate tax rate is lower in America than in every other industrialized country other than Iceland!

WAGES/BENEFITS

The average pay for a Hedge Fund Manager is $363 Million dollars per year.

Corporate profits, as a share of the entire economy, reached their highest level in more than fifty years, while the share going to wages and salaries hit a fifty-year low.

Congress again voted against increasing the minimum wage, even though it is the lowest it has been in more than fifty years relative to the cost of living, according to the Economic Policy Unit. The average full time minimum wage worker earns $10,712 a year, about $900 more than the federal poverty level for one person. It should be noted that Congress had raised its own pay over the last nine years by $31,600.

75M Americans now actually earn less per hour than in 1996.

WAR

The three main reasons for going to war were:

- Weapons of mass destruction
- Iraq's ties to September 11 terrorists
- Purchase of nuclear material from Niger

All these turned out to be false. [90]

The US is spending $9 billion a month and has spent over $300 billion total on this war, and we are losing battalions worth of casualties a month killed and injured. [91]

As T.E. Lawrence *(of Lawrence of Arabia)* said, "Arabs will always prefer a job done marginally well by an Arab, than an excellent job done by a Christian."

The above facts are intended to wake you up to the situation confronting us all in this country. Gargantuan budget and current account deficits, rising long term interest rates, sharply higher energy prices, rampant global inflationary pressures, weakening housing prices, slower corporate earnings and growth, and a rapidly declining dollar are just some of the factors that should stir your complacency into making plans for your survival in this economic storm.

To summarize, the very, very wealthy are not only getting richer, they are also getting significantly richer at the expense of those less fortunate! By reducing taxes for the wealthy and adding the expense of engaging in an unwinnable war in the Middle East, financed with a budget deficit, the economic system to which we have become accustomed may be near collapse. At the beginning, it was indicated that this was not a book about politics. Suffice it to say that the country needs to urgently consider some major changes in its foreign and domestic policies to enable rank and file citizens and their families to muster some hope for the future. The following list is not exhaustive, nor is it intended to be party-driven; it is intended as a list of priorities that are needed for this country.

CHAPTER 11

THE US NEEDS

1) A universal government-funded health care system;

2) A revised educational system that reflects the realities and needs of the New Economy with teachers who are paid accordingly;

3) A balanced budget;

4) Incentives for jobs created in this country and disincentives for jobs offshore;

5) A ban on all political contributions! (Last year lobbyists contributed $24 million to candidates in addition to 850 congressional trips worth about $4 million. Make it the end of big business and their influence on the people's government);

6) Affordable housing for the homeless; (There are 2.1 million low-income families with federal rental assistance vouchers, and 1.2 million low-income families live in public housing units with 1.5 million families on the waiting list for either vouchers or public housing);

7) Radical changes in our foreign policy toward one of containment and acceptance of other countries' desires and forms of government who present no harm to this country;

8) A significant reduction in the overall amount of money spent on the defense industries in favor of spending money on more deserving domestic programs;

9) Involvement and cooperation in programs that will reduce our dependence on foreign oil;

10) Active involvement and investment in other countries' efforts to manage global warming

CHAPTER 12

Options and Your Roadmap to a New Life

"Presume not that I am the thing I was."

– William Shakespeare,
Henry IV

CHAPTER 12

The material presented in the preceding chapters is broad in nature and represents the degree of change taking place at a global level, a national level and, of equal importance, at the individual level. It will hopefully encourage company CEO's and executives to encourage strategic change and flexibility within their organizations to make them more effective in this New Economy. However, it is equally intended that this material will help individuals make changes in their lives as needed for their future careers. To help develop your own creativity, examples of change and how various corporations were able to navigate through it and become leaders in their fields were presented. In the next chapter we present the Seven Key Steps to freedom. The material that follows summarizes some of the crucial aspects of change and how we deal with this in business and also personally. First, we must recognize that these are difficult decisions in an uncertain world.

Unfortunately those old mental models we learned are no longer going to serve us. The future will belong to those able to see forward and anticipate, and have the requisite agility to respond to whatever life may bring. Recognize patterns and connections, even though they may be incomplete, ambiguous, and conflicting. Joining the dots was a way to practice a new way of seeing, and the conclusions may be equally unfamiliar and unknown. Therefore, be open to surprises, anomalies, and unexpected findings.

Here are the key new rules that we suggest will help you in overcoming the use of familiar mental models and open your eyes to different opportunities.

1) Find new ways to spot opportunities; consider the gap between technology and what consumers want to buy.

2) Launch fast with agile teams. Use small teams and "skunk works" as pilots to test and prove new concepts.

3) Break unwritten rules. Use brainstorming or outsiders to identify ideas and innovation.

4) Outsource tasks to specialists. Sometimes outsourcers can do things better and faster by using standard technologies and components.

5) When you have it right, repeat it! Templates are ideal when something works, and you can leverage the idea elsewhere.

We trust the material presented will enable you to see that your future will be radically different from your past. This book makes the case for the importance for everyone in this country to take active steps to find his or her own personal freedom and opportunity with dignity. The following are not intended as personal answers for you but merely options worthy to consider as part of finding your own path.

OPTION 1- "IF YOU CAN'T BEAT THEM, JOIN THEM" THEORY

Many of the changes described in this book are happening through our political system; therefore, we would urge you to join a political party in some way depending on your personal desires and ambitions. You could start by registering to vote and playing an active role in the party of your choice, or even perhaps create a new political party. The country would appear to need something different and better! The country's own indifference and lack of involvement have created the situation described in this book. Change that!

Although this move will enable you to understand and be actively involved in the political process, it will not make you rich and independent – at least, not unless you become a politician of the kind already in power and now representing you! Therefore, we will consider other options to enable freedom and the opportunity to somehow share in the wealth of your company.

OPTION 2 – JOIN A "START-UP" COMPANY

The New Economy landscape will increasingly be comprised of small, fluid groups of individuals who may begin as active participants in technology but who eventually will be part of a start-up. The drive for technology appears continuous as opposed to the old style manufacturing plants, where people joined after school and stayed for their whole lives with a decent pension and benefits. Those days are gone! So if you're technology savvy and enjoy a challenge, then this option could be a better way forward for you.

Although the risks are high, typically the benefits are equally high. Most times there are stock options that enable you to share in the fruits of your labor, and although the pay may not be at as high a level as in conventional Old Economy companies, you are at least trying to change the world.

OPTION 3 – IS IT BETTER SOMEWHERE ELSE?

Many people will read this book and rightly conclude that the situation is not easily corrected and seek other places to work and live. Having lived and worked in thirteen countries, I can assure you that this is a very real option, depending on your personal situation. If this choice sounds interesting, you should get some of the many books available on your country of choice from your local library or from Agora Press, which has a number of country-specific reports ranging from Mexico to New Zealand and everywhere in between. There are also many web sites to help you in this search. **Two of the best are:**

www.escapeartist.com,
www.internationalliving.com

OPTION 4-FRANCHISES

Earlier in the book when we discussed issues and changes, we also spoke of ways in which you can make money and find the freedom you deserve in spite of the government or big business. One of the options is to buy into a franchise, which is a way in which you can own the business you want without the risk that sometimes accompanies starting a business of your own from scratch. Please note that this option is included more to complete the picture than it is out of any conviction that it might be a solution for a particular individual looking for the best to take advantage of the New Economy.

OPTION 5- THE INTERNET

We have, as they say, saved the best for last. For most individuals, the way to make money and find true freedom is to have their own business, but not just any business. The best business is one with leverage and which requires little or no time and which operates twenty-four hours a day, seven days a week, all over the world. The Internet represents the single largest opportunity for any individual to make money and find that freedom by being on the right side of the equation. This option does not require a lot of knowledge or understanding of computers or the Internet, and the next chapter will detail the seven key steps to achieving this goal.

CHAPTER 13

The Internet Blueprint Model: 7 Steps to FREEDOM in the NEW ECONOMY

"Be Great in Act, as you have been in Thought."

– William Shakespeare,
King John

CHAPTER 13

There are many books, tapes, and CDs available on this topic; however, for the most part they are practically worthless, and you should probably save your money. It's like the days of the gold rush with lots of characters attempting to sell you something you don't need. At the end of the chapter, a few contacts are listed that are known to us as being honest and providing value for money and with whom the author has personally worked.

Typically there are two choices of products in what you offer on the Internet:

a) Information products

b) Tangible products

The first of these, information products, are probably the easiest to set up. These types of products are e-books or something similar, often about solving a particular problem. These can be related to health, fitness, travel, sports, hobbies, investments, or anything that you may know something about, such as "How to Lose Weight" or "How to Quit Smoking." If this is something you have an idea for, the other steps will still apply.

STEP 1. FORM A CORPORATION.

As part of any business, including an Internet business, you should carefully consider the relative merits of forming your own corporation. There are ads in the papers and on the Internet to assist you in this. So whether you decide on a partnership, corporation, or a hybrid such as a Limited Liability Corporation (LLC), by using your new venture as a business entity you are able to protect your personal assets, and in some cases deduct the costs associated with setting up and operating your business.

Also, examine the location where your business will be headquartered. Again, we suggest you do some research on the relative merits of setting up in cities like Wilmington and being a Delaware corporation (not recommended unless you are a major corporation) and Reno, which offers many benefits including reduced taxation. Consult your attorney or tax accountant when making these important decisions. Again, if you have specific questions on incorporation, or setting up a business overseas, or general Internet/hosting technology questions, please e-mail the author.

STEP 2. FIND A HOT NICHE TARGET MARKET!

This may sound like a strange way to start rather than finding a product to sell; however, our focus is on the market, which has people who are passionate and intense about something! For example, these can be fans of Pebble Beach Golf Course, Grand Prix Formula One Racing or the Manchester United soccer team in the UK, the Rolling Stones, or jazz from a certain era, even certain hobbies or interests, as long as people are **passionate** about the subject matter.

The reason we do this rather than develop or think about a product to sell is that this audience is absolutely crazy about owning things on this subject matter. It's much easier to sell something to someone who wants what we have, **no matter what,** than offering something we might like. Luckily, there are tools to help in the search for these market niches. We will discuss two of them here as examples.

The first is **www.google.com,** and the second is **www.overture.com.** Both of these sites can help you identify a market niche, since they tell you the number of searches for a given segment of the population. For example, if you do a search on either of these search engines for their top "keyword" you'll see what people are looking for. It's also possible to go to **www.ebay.com** to see the traffic taking place there as another check on your target market. Now that you've identified the target market, you can see what people want to buy!

STEP 3. FIND WHAT THEY WANT TO BUY.

In the case of the Pebble Beach Golfing, a downloadable "hints and tips" sheet with a description of the course from a local golf professional might be something of great interest! In a case of an avid Formula One fan, something from the Monaco Grand Prix would be considered a "must-have." Look at these various market niches for clues on what you can provide them. In this way, you are making life easier to sell them something than finding a product and looking for someone to sell it to!

STEP 4. CREATE A DOMAIN NAME.

At this point you have identified a market that is passionate about their area of interest. You now need to register a domain name that will draw crowds to your web site. The choice of words should be based on words that describe the type of product you are offering. For example, use www.oaklandraidersgear.com if you are offering items that will appeal to Oakland Raiders fans. These key words are important because they also determine how the search engines rank your web site.

One suggestion is to obtain as many of the names as you can afford! This process can be done at many sites; however, www.yahoo.com offers many benefits, including a discount on the domain name registration.

STEP 5. DESIGN A WEB SITE.

Now that you have completed all the necessary components for your business, it's time to actually design the web site itself. This is not as complicated as it may appear, since there are many website designers who have templates available. For the first-time beginner, using a designer is an easy way to quickly get your website up, running, and starting to collect money. One of the best websites to help in this process is **www.godaddy.com.** They have a large number of template websites, which are fairly easy to use for someone with Internet savvy and some experience in this field. This company can also act as your hosting company for very reasonable rates. For the complete novice and beginner, please e-mail me your questions at **BarrieDay@GettingRichintheNewEconomy.com**, as we intend to provide an ongoing connection to help as many people as we can. With your help, we can determine what your needs really are and how best to help you kick-start your new career. With your feedback, we can find the tools or direct you to who will best serve you.

STEP 6. SET UP THE WEB SITE AND START COLLECTING THE MONEY!

With the web site up and a catchy domain name to match, you are effectively in business; however, like any business, you have to draw people to your site. One way to do this is to offer something free. It can be a downloadable e-booklet or a free subscription to your services. Just remember, people love something that's free or to feel that they received a deal. When starting out you have to consider the types of clients and how they might want to pay. The service at **www.paypal.com** is an excellent method for making payments because it guarantees that payments are secure and because it permits you to accept credit cards.

STEP 7. CONSIDER OTHER REVENUE OPPORTUNITIES.

Now you're actively in business, and you've done all you can to market your web site. It's time to consider other revenue opportunities. For example, if you are offering Pebble Beach information products, it might be beneficial to offer other golf club memorabilia or provide a schedule of tournaments. The important part is to consider who and what can be an additional source of revenue. What you're trying to achieve is to have people who visit your site spend as much as possible with you. Therefore, those sites that offer a diverse range of products will be the most successful. By having links both to and from your site you will also raise your ratings in the search engines. If you can, find something to add on a consistent basis, since this will also impact your rating. A simple newsletter can be enough to let people know what you're trying to do.

FINALLY!

At this point, you're probably thinking, "Wow! This sounds great, and it's so easy." Well, like any business, it still depends on the right marketing tools coupled with the right product. There are many related books on the market to help you with setting up your web site, and if you go to my web site **www. GettingRichintheNewEconomy.com** , there is additional reference material to help you further.

CHAPTER 14

Final Thoughts

"I wish you well, and so I take my leave,
I pray you know me when we meet again."

– William Shakespeare,
Merchant of Venice

CHAPTER 14

The material presented in the preceding chapters can be perceived as negative or discouraging; however, it is a potpourri of some of the major issues the country faces and should encourage you to make major changes in how you think and what you do. People are powerful, and the human spirit is able to move through these issues; therefore, it is possible for you to make money and enjoy life in the New Economy. I live in a small town, but I have been struck by the individuals who have created something, sometimes from nothing, even in these difficult times.

For example, take Stacey Belkin who owns Stacy's Restaurant on Main Street in Pleasanton, California. Stacey is a young woman who, until April 1998, was working as a restaurant manager when one of her regular patrons, Scott Adams, asked her to present him with a business plan for a place of her own. In Scott's words, it "weeded out the dreamers from the doers."

What she gave him was a complete restaurant business plan. Eighteen months later, in 1997, Stacey's Cafe was born. Stacy has now expanded to include two restaurants: one Stacey's at Waterford in Dublin, California, as well as the original Stacey's in downtown Pleasanton. Stacey still keeps the original scrap of paper with Scott Adams' phone number as a reminder that actions speak louder than dreams.

Another of our real life heroes is Marty Metro, founder and president of a startup called UsedCardboardBoxes.com in Los Angeles, California. Marty developed a business model to enable the purchase and re-use of cardboard boxes at half price to consumers. This recycled leverage-approach benefited both customers and the environment. With ten years of corporate experience in computer systems and technology consulting, Marty had known success; but this innovative idea forced him to leave the corporate world and trade in his BMW (sports edition, no less) for a delivery truck!

With a simple web site and a vision, Marty was able to grow his business into a national brand offering franchises across the country. In the first two years his company was dealing with 5,000 customer orders! Like any start-up, Marty encountered problems, mainly by trying to do everything himself, including financing the business with his personal credit cards! However, the business has matured over the last two years, and so has Marty. Armed with the knowledge and experience gained in this business, he is ready for further dynamic growth. It wasn't this way in the beginning. Many "pooh-poohed" the idea, but luckily others disagreed, including private investors and venture capitalists who wanted a share of the dream and were willing to put their money behind it in exchange for a piece of the action.

The inspiration, like many of our other heroes, comes from their attitude towards life:

- Be oblivious to the doom and gloom nay-sayers!
- Hold onto your dreams!
- And…never, ever be satisfied with the status quo!

Steve and Jillian McAlpine are owners of the Luggage Store in Carmel, California. Back in 1991 they were operating out of their home in Stockton, California, running a small but successful storefront luggage business, in spite of the recession and the Gulf War that was affecting the country.

In February 1995 they moved to Carmel to open the Luggage Store in the Cross Roads Shopping Center and spent the next three and one-half years commuting to Stockton to help their daughters run the original store. When the Carmel store opened on March 10, 1995, the second flood in over one hundred years struck Carmel, and many store owners had to be evacuated! On that memorable first day, the McAlpines were wondering if they had made the right choice. The weather was awful, and they had not made a dime on that first day of business.

However, like many of the other successful entrepreneurs described in this chapter they stuck to their fundamental beliefs in their vision and chose to expand, and in fact they doubled their retail space from 1700 square feet to almost 3300 square feet. This was at a time when the economy was going through a recession and five competing luggage stores were forced out of business in the area. It is noteworthy that sixty percent of the industry at that time went under! It was also nine months before 9/11 took place!

Today, in spite of all the preceding events, Steve and Jillian have created a successful and profitable business. **The secret of their success, like so many of the other heroes described in this chapter, can be summarized as:**

- Do your homework and don't open a business on a whim!

- Be prepared to work twice as hard as you ever did before!

- Give it your all!

- The only thing you have to sell in business is service, so make sure that every customer has a great experience, every time!

- Get excited about what you're doing, and make sure your staff feels the same way!

- Do not let others discourage you from your dreams!

If you're in the area, stop by to see and experience this great American success story for yourself!

These people had vision, innovation, passion, and persistence! What's happening in your town? Can you find other entrepreneurs like yourself just waiting for the right moment? If not, maybe you need to find like-minded people.

In conclusion please enjoy the following:

A Japanese company and an American company decided to have a canoe race on the Mississippi River. Both teams practiced long and hard to reach their peak performance before the race.

On the big day, the Japanese won by a mile. The Americans, very discouraged and depressed, decided to form a team made up of senior managers to investigate the reasons they lost and to recommend appropriate action. Their conclusion was the Japanese had eight people rowing and one person steering, while the American team had eight people steering and one person rowing.

So American management hired a consulting company and paid them a large amount of money for a second opinion. They advised that too many people were steering the boat, while not enough people were rowing. To prevent another loss to the Japanese, the rowing team's management structure was totally reorganized to four steering supervisors, three area steering superintendents and one assistant superintendent steering manager. They also implemented a new performance system that would give the one person rowing the boat greater incentive to work harder. It was called the "Rowing Team Quality First Program," and they held meetings, attended dinners, and offered free pens for the rower. They discussed getting new paddles, canoes, and other equipment, they considered extra vacation days for practices, and they developed a bonus plan based on performance.

The next year the Japanese won by two miles. Humiliated, the American management laid off the rower for poor performance, halted development of a new canoe, sold the paddles, and canceled all capital investments for new equipment. The money saved was distributed to the senior executives as bonuses, and the next year's racing team was outsourced to India.

If this reminds you of where you're working, leave now!
Good Luck! Let us know how you're doing.

Sincerely
– **Barrie Day**

ABOUT THE AUTHOR

Barrie Day is CEO and Managing Partner of Enterprise Technology Solutions; LLC, a Palo Alto based global High Technology Consulting & Change management Company for Fortune 500 clients. He is a graduate of the University of California and Stanford and is an internationally recognized consultant who has worked with CEOs of major corporations as a trusted advisor in start-ups and business turnarounds. His clients have included Apple Computer, DuPont, Philips Netherlands, Nortel, ITT, America On-Line, Smith & Nephew Ltd., Mercury Communications UK, Microsoft, Coca Cola, and many others. He has been helping clients radically improve their business operations with innovation in the areas of strategy, systems, processes, organization, and cultural change for over twenty years.

Barrie has lived and worked in thirteen countries and speaks fluent Dutch, French, and German. He has started and managed many successful businesses and has lectured extensively at conferences and seminars around the world on technology, along with the need for organizational and cultural change as part of effective business transformation. He is highly experienced in reading corporate cultures and the dynamics of change; therefore, he has been invited by numerous Fortune 500 companies and boards of management to assist them in making major transformations. He has interacted with people at the executive level and can work equally effectively with people in plants or on the shop floor. Barrie communicates openly, honestly, and objectively. These skills and strengths have proven successful in helping large corporations where fresh, unbiased and honest assessments of the situation are essential. He brings experience, dedication, courage, tenacity and enthusiasm to any situation.

Barrie is an avid ocean going sailor, and his interests include travel, art, gourmet food, fine wine, photography, jazz, cricket, Monty Python, and Formula One racing cars. He divides his time between Palo Alto, California, and Europe. He can be contacted directly by emailing him at barrieday@GettingRichintheNewEconomy.com.

APPENDIX

The Best Corporations in the New Economy

"They well deserve to have, that know the strong'st and surest way to get."

– William Shakespeare,
Richard II

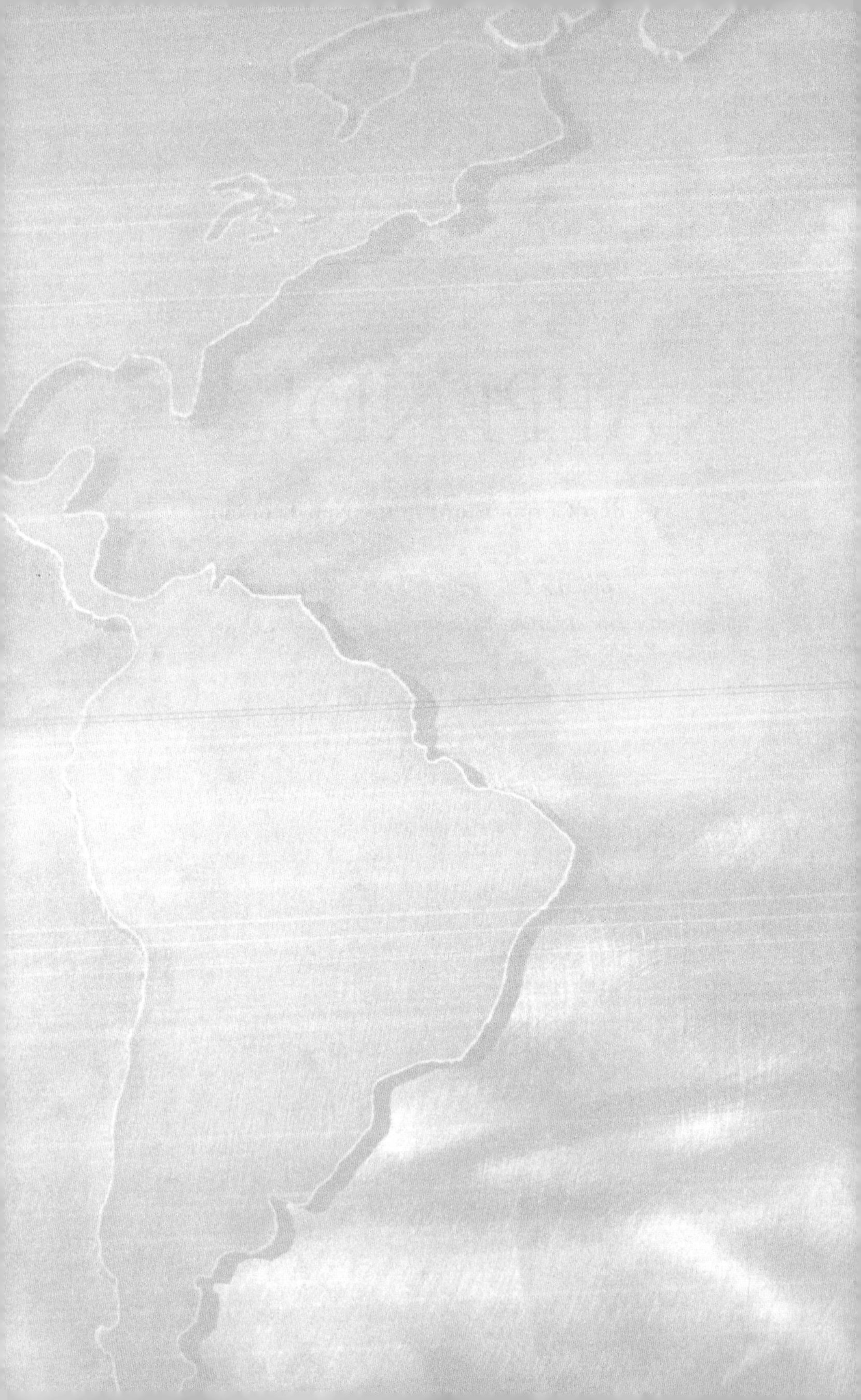

FedEx Corporation (www.fedex.com) NYSE (FDX)

942 South Shady Grove Road, Memphis, TN 38120
Ph: (901) 818 7500 Fax: (901) 818 7388

(All figures in Millions except EPS)	2005	2004	2003
Net Sales	**29,363.00**	**24,710.00**	**22,487.00**
Cost of Goods Sold	13,467.00	10,732.00	9,889.00
EBITDA	3,933.00	3,250.00	2,820.00
Net Income	1,449.00	838.00	830.00
Diluted EPS (Total)	4.72	4.19	2.74
Cash at Beginning of Period	1,046.00	538.00	331.00
Cash at End of Period	1,039.00	1,046.00	538.00

Recognized as one of Fortune Magazine's top 100 best companies to work for, the 9th consecutive time, today FedEx is a group of $29.0 billion dollar group of companies specializing in transportation and business solutions targeted specifically towards the e-business era. The company enjoys a wide international presence by being present in 220 countries and a combined employee and contractor base of 260,000 employees. As stated on the company website, the group is divided into seven main categories of business. They are FedEx Express, FedEx Ground, FedEx Freight, FedEx Kinko's, FedEx Trade Services, FedEx Supply Chain Management and FedEx Custom Critical. The Express, Ground and Freight are courier solutions and also most commonly used by an average consumer. FedEx Kinko's provides complete business and document solutions to its client base.

Financial highlights: 200 Annual Report

GOOGLE INC (www.google.com) Nasdaq (GOOG)

1600 Amphitheatre Parkway, Mountain View, CA 94043
Ph: (650) 253 4000, Fax: (650) 618 1499

(All figures in Millions except EPS)	2005	2004	2003
Net Sales	**6,138.56**	**3,189.22**	**1,465.93**
Cost of Goods Sold	2,571.51	1,457.65	625.85
EBITDA	2,401.09	989.67	397.51
Net Income	1,465.40	399.12	105.65
Diluted EPS (Total)	5.02	1.46	0.41
Cash at Beginning of Period	426.87	149.00	57.75
Cash at End of Period	3,877.17	426.87	149.00

Google Inc. is ranked and recognized as the most efficient search engine. The Bay area company has the reputation for hiring the best, and as of Dec 2005 has an employee base of 5300 employees. Google offers its users the capability to search information online freely through many international domains with the most popular one being www.google.com . Its main source of revenue is through online advertising in the form of its Ad Words program. In addition to providing search engine services free of charge, the company also offers Gmail (Google email), Maps, and Google Desktop and many other services free to its client base.

Financial highlights: 2005 highlights

YAHOO INC (www.yahoo.com) Nasdaq (YHOO)

701 First Avenue, Sunnyvale, CA 94089
Ph: (408) 349 3300, Fax: (408) 349 3301

(All figures in Millions except EPS)	2005	2004	2003
Net Sales	**5,257.76**	**3,574.52**	**1,625.10**
Cost of Goods Sold	2,096.20	1,298.56	358.10
EBITDA	1,504.87	999.62	455.35
Net Income	1,896.23	839.55	237.88
Diluted EPS (Total)	1.28	0.58	0.18
Cash at Beginning of Period	823.72	415.89	234.07
Cash at End of Period	1,429.69	823.72	415.89

What started as a hobby has today evolved into one of the most successful companies of the internet era. Yahoo has evolved from a simple database of popular websites to a global network of interconnected services ranging from a search engine, marketplace, communications, commerce and online advertising. Headquartered in Sunnyvale, CA the company has offices in Europe, Asia-Pacific, Latin America and Canada. Yahoo has and continues to be Google's prime competitor. While revenues are comparable, take note of the difference in the cash situation of the two companies.

Financial highlights:2005 Annual Report

WAL-MART STORES, INC. (www.Wal-Mart.com) NYSE (WMT)

Wal-Mart Stores Inc., Bentonville, Arkansas 72716
Customer: 1 800 WAL MART; Investor/Analyst: 479 273 8446;
Journalist: 479 273 4314

(All figures in Millions except EPS)	2005	2004	2003
Net Sales	**5,257.76**	**3,574.52**	**1,625.10**
Cost of Goods Sold	2,096.20	1,298.56	358.10
EBITDA	1,504.87	999.62	455.35
Net Income	1,896.23	839.55	237.88
Diluted EPS (Total)	1.28	0.58	0.18
Cash at Beginning of Period	823.72	415.89	234.07
Cash at End of Period	1,429.69	823.72	415.89

Wal-Mart is synonymous to retail shopping. Sam Walton's dream was to give "his customers what they want" at the least possible price. And Wal-Mart today has achieved that through its superior supply chain management system, through its capability to foster unique relationships with its suppliers and most importantly by trying to look at it from the customers perspective. Headquarted in Bentonville, Arkansas Wal-Mart employs 1.3 million associates and manages more than 5000 stores across fifteen countries. Wal-Mart continues to give its customer the best value for money by cost reductions at the supplier level.

Financial highlights:2005 Annual Report

SOUTHWEST AIRLINES CO. (www.southwest.com) NYSE (LUV)

702 Love Field Drive, Dallas, Texas 75235
HQ Main Switchboard: (214) 792 4000;
Investor/Analyst: (214) 792 4415; Journalist: (214) 792 4847

(All figures in Millions except EPS)	2005	2004	2003
Net Sales	**7,584.00**	**6,530.00**	**5,937.00**
Cost of Goods Sold	3,593.00	3,100.00	2,798.00
EBITDA	1,322.00	1,021.00	900.00
Net Income	548.00	313.00	442.00
Diluted EPS (Total)	0.67	0.38	0.54
Cash at Beginning of Period	1,048.00	1,484.00	1,815.00
Cash at End of Period	2,280.00	1,048.00	1,484.00

With its first flight more than thirty-four years ago, Southwest Airlines today is America's leading discount airline. It is also the only airline that has been able to ride the tough times profitably without declaring bankruptcy or employee layoffs. Built on the philosophy of recognizing its employees as an asset, the airline employees 31,000 individuals across its system, and flies to 62 cities within in 32 states across The United States.

Financial highlights: Southwest Airlines - Investor Relations

APPLE COMPUTERS. (www.apple.com) **Nasdaq (AAPL)**

1 Infinite Loop, Cupertino, CA 95014
Ph: (408) 996 1010 Fax: (408) 974 2113

(All figures in Millions except EPS)	2005	2004	2003
Net Sales	**13,931.00**	**8,279.00**	**6,207.00**
Cost of Goods Sold	9,888.00	6,020.00	4,499.00
EBITDA	1,829.00	499.00	138.00
Net Income	1,335.00	276.00	69.00
Diluted EPS (Total)	1.56	0.36	0.09
Cash at Beginning of Period	2,969.00	3,396.00	2,252.00
Cash at End of Period	3,491.00	2,969.00	3,396.00

Apple Computers is what I like to call the mystery company. It has an excellent and superior product,but success has always played hide and seek with the company until recently. In the business of designing, manufacturing and marketing PC's and related software and accessories, Apple has come back into the game with the launch of iPOD. Notice that the increase in revenue numbers coincides with the continued increasing popularity of the iPOD. With its initial public offering in 1980 and the intense competition Apple continues to maintain a respectable stock price within the industry, this is further proof to its superior line of products. Despite a 68% increase in revenue over 2004, the difference between Apple and Dell is astonishing.

Financial highlights: Apple 5 Year Financials

DELL INC. (www.dell.com) Nasdaq (DELL)

One Dell Way, Round Rock, Texas 78682
Ph: (512) 338 4400 Fax: (512) 728 4238
Investors: (512) 728 7800 Media: (512) 728 4100

(All figures in Millions except EPS)	2005	2004	2003
Net Sales	**49,205.00**	**41,444.00**	**35,404.00**
Cost of Goods Sold	40,190.00	33,892.00	29,055.00
EBITDA	4,588.00	3,807.00	3,055.00
Net Income	3,323.00	2,645.00	2,122.00
Diluted EPS (Total)	1.29	1.01	0.80
Cash at Beginning of Period	4,747.00	4,317.00	4,232.00
Cash at End of Period	7,042.00	4,747.00	4,317.00

Dell Inc. has and will be a business model that many will continue to try and duplicate. Dell designs and builds customized solutions for a wide customer base ranging from college students to multi-location businesses. In addition to Inspiron Notebooks and Dimension desk tops the range of products also includes Dell PowerEdge servers, PowerVault and Dell EMC storage systems. Additionally, they also offer complementary products such as printers and projectors. The initial contact point for a Dell customer is its website through which the customers can either design their product or contact a relevant department. Considering the sheer size of their business, it has separate phone lines for businesses, schools, government offices etc. With 65,200 employees worldwide, Dell has international manufacturing facilities in Brazil, China, Ireland and Malaysia. Its largest facility in global operations started in the fall of 2005 at Winston-Salem, N.C

Financial highlights: Financial History

Ebay Inc. (www.ebay.com) **Nasdaq (Ebay)**

2145 Hamilton Avenue, San Jose CA 95125
Ph: (408) 558 7400 Fax: (408) 369 4855
Customer: (888) 749 3229 or (800) 322 9266

(All figures in Millions except EPS)	2005	2004	2003
Net Sales	**4,552.40**	**3,271.30**	**2,165.10**
Cost of Goods Sold	818.10	614.42	416.06
EBITDA	1,851.64	1,318.76	818.21
Net Income	1,082.04	778.22	441.77
Diluted EPS (Total)	0.78	0.57	0.34
Cash at Beginning of Period	1,330.15	1,381.51	1,109.31
Cash at End of Period	1,313.58	1,330.15	1,381.51

What started off as an auction site for hard to find items, is today an online marketplace for everything,,including used cars. The website promotes a rating system that helps keep fraudulent activities at check. The recent partnership announcement between eBay and Yahoo is yet another step by the two companies to create synergy across its value chain. The partnership agreement will essentially focus on search and graphical advertising, online payments, click to call and a co-branded tool bar on eBay, which will include Yahoo services such as Yahoo! mail and My Yahoo!(eBay News: Yahoo! and eBay Form Strategic Partnership to Further Expand Their Businesses in U.S.) With an employee base of 11,600, eBay enjoys an international customer base through its 27 country specific website accessible from either www.ebay.com.

Financial highlights: eBay - Annual Reports

Amazon.com Inc. (www.amazon.com) Nasdaq (AMZN)

12th Avenue South, Suite 1200, Seattle, WA 98144
Ph: (206) 266 1000 Fax: (206) 622 2405

(All figures in Millions except EPS)	2005	2004	2003
Net Sales	**8,490.00**	**6,921.00**	**5,263.70**
Cost of Goods Sold	6,451.00	5,319.00	4,006.53
EBITDA	553.00	516.00	349.05
Net Income	359.00	588.00	35.28
Diluted EPS (Total)	0.84	1.39	0.08
Cash at Beginning of Period	1,303.00	1,102.00	738.25
Cash at End of Period	1,013.00	1,303.00	1,102.00

A single man's ambition to create the "Earth's most customer centric company" Amazon.com started with only one product –books. Its founder Jeff Bezos believed that the internet had and offered the potential to create a very unique environment for its users to browse and purchase both popular and hard to find books by sitting in the comfort of their homes. Today, Amazon.com has expanded its product to line to thirty two categories including grocery, clothing and a wider range of consumer goods. With an employee base of 12,000 both full time and part time employees globally, Amazon.com enjoys and international presence by having websites unique to France, Germany, UK, Japan, Canada and China. It also has fulfillment and customer service centers in Europe and Asia.

Financial highlights: Amazon.com Investor Relations: Historical Financials

WebMD. (www.webmd.com) **Nasdaq (WBMD)**

111 8th Avenue, 7th Floor, NY 10011
Ph: (212) 624 3700 Investor/ Analyst: (212) 624 3817
Media: (212) 624 3700

(All figures in Millions except EPS)	2005	2004	2003
Net Sales	**168.94**	**134.15**	**110.15**
Cost of Goods Sold	70.54	52.38	47.00
EBITDA	17.09	12.29	(2.78)
Net Income	7.75	6.46	(7.43)
Diluted EPS (Total)	0.15	0.13	(0.15)
Cash at Beginning of Period	3.46	0.36	0.15
Cash at End of Period	75.70	3.46	0.36

WebMD is the common man's answer to complex medical questions that can be a dilemma to understand. It provides insightful medical information in easy to understand language that enables its users to better educate themselves and make more informed decisions. Additionally, it provides subscription-based services to medical providers and also assists in maintaining medical databases. One of its most valuable tools from a consumer perspective is the "community" feature that allows individuals to share experiences and hence provide e-support or online support to each other.

Financial highlights: No Info on website.

AMERICA ONLINE. (www.aol.com) NYSE (TWX)

Time Warner Inc., One Time Warner Center, New York, NY 10019
Ph: (212) 484 8000 Fax: (212) 489 6183

(All figures in Millions except EPS)	2005	2004	2003
Net Sales	**43,652.00**	**42,089.00**	**39,563.00**
Subscription	22,222	21,605	20,488
Advertising	7,612	6,955	6,180
Content	12,615	12,350	11,446
Other	1,203	1,179	1,489
Cost of Goods Sold	25,075.00	24,449.00	23,422.00
EBITDA	14,292.00	12,846.00	11,390.00
Net Income	2,905.00	3,364.00	2,639.00
Diluted EPS (Total)	0.62	0.72	0.57
Cash at Beginning of Period	6,139.00	3,040.00	1,730.00
Cash at End of Period	4,220.00	6,139.00	3,040.00

A division of Time Warner Inc., America Online eliminated the education gap between different users of the internet. Aggressive marketing in the form of AOL CD's and ease of use increased its customer base initially. Later, a few management errors and the increased popularity of Yahoo decreased its base. The company does not provide any financial information on its website. Hence, the numbers above have been taken from the Time Warner annual report. Also, there is no specific contact information for AOL on its website.

Financial highlights: Annual Report : FS

MONSTER WORLDWIDE INC. (www.monster.com) Nasdaq (MNST)

622 Third Avenue, New York, NY 10017
Ph: (212) 351 7000 Fax: (646) 658 0541
Job Seekers / Employers: 1 800 MONSTER

(All figures in Millions except EPS)	2005	2004	2003
Net Sales	**986.92**	**756.13**	**552.10**
Cost of Goods Sold	(37.96)	(33.03)	(23.35)
EBITDA	214.37	131.57	27.51
Net Income	107.43	73.10	(81.86)
Diluted EPS (Total)	0.86	0.61	(0.73)
Cash at Beginning of Period	198.11	142.26	165.65
Cash at End of Period	196.60	198.11	145.26

Monster.com is a part of the Monster Worldwide and provides access into the business of providing business training and employment services to both job seekers and employers. It has an employee base of 4,800 employees and is present in 20 countries. In addition to providing resume search and job matching, the company also provides HR solutions to businesses.

Financial highlights: Link through website n/a

FOOTNOTES

FOOTNOTES

1) http://www.cincypost.com/business/2000/nasdaq030800.html

2) www.fool.com : Amazon and Amgen Report [Rule Breaker], July 26, 2000

3) http://www.post-gazette.com/pg/06023/643018.stm : Amazon.com Ends Relationship with Circuit City.

4) http://www.thestandard.com/article/0,1902,27911,00.html : Webvan & Bankruptcy.

5) Wall Street Journal (12/15/2005), "Wal-Mart's H-P Elves"

6) Wall Street Journal (12/19/05), "Keeping Ahead of the Pack"

7) Goleman, Daniel. Business, The Ultimate Resource , Perseus Publishing, ISBN: 0-7382-0242-8

8) http://inventors.about.com/library/inventors/blscotchtape.htm

9) http://www.greatachievements.org: History of Internet and how it evolved.

10) http://yhoo.client.shareholder.com/press/timeline.cfm

11) http://archives.cnn.com/2000/TECH/computing/02/02/aol.lawsuit.02/

12) http://news.com.com/2100-1023-235400.html: AOL Time Warner Merger.

13) www.USATODAY.com : FedEx Chief Takes Cue from Leaders in History.

14) www.Walmart.com

15) www.Walmart.com

16) http://www.internetretailer.com/IR2006/agenda.asp

17) http://mitworld.mit.edu/video/1/

18) PR Newswire, June 10, 1997

19) http://mitworld.mit.edu/video/1/

20) http://en.wikipedia.org/wiki/Pierre_Omidyar

21) http://www.forbes.com/2006/01/19/ebay-earnings-0119markets17.html?partner=msn

22) http://www.census.gov/ipc/www/popclockworld.html

23) http://formums.ebay.com : History of eBay.

24) http://www.businessweek.com/magazine/content/01_49/b3760605.htm

25) http://en.wikipedia.org/wiki/Pierre_Omidyar

26) http://www.macobserver.com/columns/appletrader/00/000821.shtml : Apple Computers and Superiority of their Products.

27) www.bestbuy.com

28) http://money.cnn.com/2006/01/10/technology/apple/index.htm

FOOTNOTES

29) www.USATODAY.com : Dell Business Model Turns to Muscle as Rivals Struggle.

30) http://www.usatoday.com/money/industries/technology/2003-01-19-dell-cover_x.htm

31) http://seattletimes.nwsource.com/html/businesstechnology/2002772732_airlines31.html

32) http://money.cnn.com/2005/07/14/news/fortune500/southwest/index.htm

33) http://airlines.ws/: Rating of Southwest.

34) www.southwest.com : 2004 Annual Report.

35) www.USATODAY.com : Southwest First Airline to Offer Free Travel to Independence Air Customers.

36) www.achievement .org : Frederick W. Smith Biography.

37) www.fedex.com

38) http://en.wikipedia.org/wiki/Spoke-hub_distribution_paradigm

39) http://news.com.com/2100-1011_3-5134056.html: FedEx/Kinko's.

40) http://www.usps.com/mailerscompanion/mayjune2004/mc0604art8.htm : USPS - FedEx Alliance.

41) www.WSJ.com : FedEx Takes Control of its China Business.

42) http://www.usatoday.com/money/companies/management/2005-06-19-fedex-advice_x.htm

43) www.CNET News.com : Healtheon Shares Jump on WebMD Deal.

44) http://news.com.com/Diagnosing+WebMD/2009-1017_3-5208510.html : WEBMD Analysis.

45) http://www.internetnews.com/ec-news/article.php/728311 : Pfizer Attempt to Organize the Industry – WebMD competition.

46) http://phx.corporate-ir.net/phoenix.zhtml?c=189524&p=irol-newsArticle&ID=805734&highlight= WebMD purchase of eMedicine.com, Inc.

47) website www.myfoodphone.com

48) www.indystar.com : Carmel Tech Firm, by Daniel Lee, 2/9/06

49) http://www.thestreet.com/markets/marketfeatures/889679.html

50) http://www.bea.gov/bea/newsrel/transnewsrelease.htm

51) http://www.epinet.org/content.cfm/webfeatures_econindicators_tradepict20060210: Trade Picture.

52) http://www.epinet.org/content.cfm/webfeatures_econindicators_tradepict20060210

53) http://www.economist.com/displaystory.cfm?story_id=5176103

54) www.thenation.com/doc/20010723/klare

FOOTNOTES

55) www.ppionline.org : Ill Wind From China: Rapid Growth Brings Pollution, Higher Gas Prices by Jan Mazurek.

56) www.ppionline.org : DLC: Idea of the Week: Responding to China's Power Surge.

57) http://times.hanooki.com : The Korea Times : Korea Ranks 49th on World Happiness Scale.

58) http://en.wikipedia.org/wiki/Gross_national_happiness

59) http://www.rediff.com : US, China, India: A tri-polar World?

60) http://nationalpriorities.org : Proposed Discretionary Budget, FY2007 Request.

61) http://nationalpriorities.org : National Security.

62) http://www.Economist.com : The Quadrennial Defense Review, Rummy's Wish List .

63) www.whitehouse.gov : 2007 Analytical Perspectives, page 184

64) http://www.cbpp.org : A "Mere" $300 Billion: Should a $300 Billion Deficit Be Considered a Victory?, Revised 6/5/06.

65) http://www.Economist.com : The Economics of Saving, The shift Away from Thrift.

66) www.whitehouse.gov : Analytical Perspectives, FY 2007.

67) http://www.whitehouse.gov/omb/budget/fy2007

68) www.whitehouse.gov : Analytical Perspectives, FY 2007.

69) http://www.epinet.org/content.cfm/bp156: Economic Policy Institute, Briefing Paper: Collision course: The Bush Budget and Social Security.

70) Trustees, 2004

71) http://www.wsj.com/article : Health Care Plan

72) www.bls.gov and www.census.gov

73) http://www.Economist.com : Economics Focus, Myths and Migration.

74) http://www.washingtonpost.com : Immigration Reform Proposals

75) http://blog.aflcio.org : Unions Need to Find New Ways to Organize Immigrant Workers.

76) http://www.Economist.com : The Public Mood, The Isolationist Temptation.

77) Economic Perspectives, Vol. 29

78) http://balitmorechronicle.com : February 13, 2006, Nuking the Economy

79) http://www.chicagofed.org/publications/economicperspectives/ep_2qtr2005_part3_lynch.pdf

80) http://www.nytimes.com : June 6, 2004, When Sweet Statistics Clash With a Sour Mood

FOOTNOTES

81) http://www.igt.com/articles/2005/01/06/business/cars.php

82) Unknown author

83) USA Today, October 27, 2006.

84) Time Magazine

85) New York Times, April 13 2006, "The Health of a Nation

86) Report by America's Health Insurance Trade Group March 9 2006

87) Study, Harvard University

88) USA Today, May 2006

89) USA Today, October 27, 2006

90) San Francisco Chronicle, March 22, 2006, Report on a Cleveland City Club Republican event.

91) USA Today, March 19, 2006

Share This Message

Bulk Discounts

Discounts start at a low number of copies, ranging from 30% to 50% off based on the quantity chosen.

Custom Publishing

Would you like a private label? or a customization to suit your needs. We could even highlight specific chapters.

Sponsorship

Would you like to sponsor this book? It's a great way to advertise your product or service in a unique way!

Dynamic Speakers

Authors are available to you, to share their expertise at your event!

Call LifeSuccess Publishing at 1-800-473-7134 or email info@lifesuccesspublishing.com for more information

LIFE SUCCESS PUBLISHING

OTHER BOOKS FROM LIFESUCCESS PUBLISHING

You Were Born Rich

Bob Proctor
ISBN # 978-0-9656264-1-5

The Millionaire Mindset
How Ordinary People Can Create Extraordinary Income

Gerry Robert
ISBN # 978-1-59930-030-6

Rekindle The Magic In Your Relationship
Making Love Work

Anita Jackson
ISBN # 978-1-59930-041-2

Finding The Bloom of The Cactus Generation
Improving the quality of life for Seniors

Maggie Walters
ISBN # 978-1-59930-011-5

The Beverly Hills Shape
The Truth About Plastic Surgery

Dr. Stuart Linder
ISBN # 978-1-59930-049-8

Wellness Our Birthright
How to give a baby the best start in life.

Vivien Clere Green
ISBN # 978-1-59930-020-7

Lighten Your Load

Peter Field
ISBN # 978-1-59930-000-9

Change & How To Survive In The New Economy
7 steps to finding freedom & escaping the rat race

Barrie Day
ISBN # 978-1-59930-015-3

OTHER BOOKS FROM LIFESUCCESS PUBLISHING

Stop Singing The Blues
10 Powerful Strategies For Hitting The High Notes In Your Life

Dr. Cynthia Barnett
ISBN # 978-1-59930-022-1

Don't Be A Victim,
Protect Yourself
Everything Seniors Need To Know To Avoid Being Taken Financially

Jean Ann Dorrell
ISBN # 978-1-59930-024-5

A "Hand Up", not a "Hand Out"
The best ways to help others help themselves

David Butler
ISBN # 978-1-59930-071-9

Doctor Your Medicine Is Killing Me!
One Mans Journey From Near Death to Health and Wellness

Pete Coussa
ISBN # 978-1-59930-047-4

I Believe in Me
7 Ways for Woman to Step Ahead in Confidence

Lisa Gorman
ISBN # 978-1-59930-069-6

The Color of Success
Why Color Matters in your Life, your Love, your Lexus

Mary Ellen Lapp
ISBN # 978-1-59930-078-8

If Not Now, When?
What's Your Dream?

Cindy Nielsen
ISBN # 978-1-59930-073-3

The Skills to Pay the Bills... and then some!
How to inspire everyone in your organisation into high performance!

Buki Mosaku
ISBN # 978-1-59930-058-0

OTHER BOOKS FROM LIFESUCCESS PUBLISHING

The Secret To Cracking
The Property Code
7 Timeless Principles for Successful Real Estate Investment

Richard S.G. Poole
ISBN # 978-1-59930-063-4

Why My Mother Didn't Want Me To Be Psychic
The Intelligent Guide To The Sixth Sense

Heidi Sawyer
ISBN # 978-1-59930-052-8

The Make It Happen Ma
10 ways to turn obstacles into stepping stones without breaking a sweat

Dean Storer
ISBN # 978-1-59930-077-1

Change your body
Change your life
with the Fittest Couple in the World

Matt Thom &
Monica Wright
ISBN # 978-1-59930-065-8

Good Vibrations!
Can you tune in to a more positive life?

Clare Tonkin
ISBN # 978-1-59930-064-1

The Millionaire Genius
How to wake up the money magic within you.

David Ogunnaike
ISBN # 978-1-59930-026-9

Scoring Eagles
Improve Your Score In Golf, Business and Life

Max Carbone
ISBN # 978-1-59930-045-0

The Einstein Complex
Awaken your inner genius, live your dream.

Dr. Roger A. Boger
ISBN # 978-1-59930-055-9

OTHER BOOKS FROM LIFESUCCESS PUBLISHING

Break Through to You
How to Change Your World Through the Power of You!

Lisa Watson
ISBN # 978-1-59930-084-9

The Pendulum of Life
Unleash the Creative Power of Your Mind

Marcus Freudenmann
ISBN # 978-1-59930-075-7

The Sweet Smell of Success
Health & Wealth Secrets

James "Tad" Geiger M.D.
ISBN # 978-1-59930-088-7

Living the Law of Attraction
Real Stories of People Manifesting Wealth, Health and Happiness

Rich German, Andy Wong & Robin Hoch
ISBN # 978-1-59930-091-7

Wealth Matters
Abundance is Your Birthlight

Chris J. Snook with Chet Snook
ISBN # 978-1-59930-096-2

The Success Toolbox
For Entrepreneurs

Janis Vos
ISBN # 978-1-59930-005-4

Chemical Free Kids
Raising Healthy Children in a Toxic World

Dr. Sarah Lantz
ISBN # 978-1-59930-072-6

The Girlz Guide to Building Wealth
...and men like it too

Maya Galletta, Aaron Cohen, Polly McCormick, Mike McCormick
ISBN # 978-1-59930-048-1